DYNAMIC HEALTH

To Gavin
with every good
wish.

Dan Hegarty
march 2007

First published in 1997 by
Marino Books

This edition by
Life Dynamics, 2005
53 Middle Abbey Street
Dublin 1

Trade enquiries to above

C David Hegarty 2005.

ISBN   0-9548239 - 0 - 7

A CIP record for this title is available
from the British Library

Illustrations by Mark Tobin
Cover Design by Tom Keegan
Set by Tom Keegan
Printed in Ireland by ColourBooks,
Baldoyle Industrial Estate,Dublin 13

DYNAMIC HEALTH

DAVID HEGARTY

ABOUT THE AUTHOR

David Hegarty has practised the principles he talks about.

In his youth he studied and practised many of the disciplines of fitness. In 1969 he turned a consuming interest into a career and entered the fledgling industry.

He married Françoise, his French wife in 1972, and they opened their own fitness centre in 1973.

In 1974 he established and developed the Yogametric system. His enthusiasm for this system stems from his total belief in its efficacy, a belief founded on the results he has seen women and men from fifteen to eighty achieve from it over the years.

Through the years, he has persevered in developing the system, simplifying and modifying wherever possible. Now he has, he believes, an efficient and practical way for anyone to become fit and healthy.

David Hegarty's belief is that fitness is more than fast exercise and diet, but a system in which body, mind, heart and soul all find nourishment for a happier, healthier life.

He has contributed to radio programmes, written countless articles and had three works of fiction published.

CONTENTS

INTRODUCTION

The seeds of this book were sown over fifty-one years ago. I was a healthy active ten-year-old. Friends, school, family and sporting activity were the cornerstones of my existence.

Until the pleurisy.

It hit after a couple of unacknowledged warnings: severe stitches, extreme pain during exertion, night sweats, sleep-less-ness, fatigue. The crisis came on a wet November Sunday, late at night. By the early hours of Monday morning Dr Tom McCabe had been called to the house. I recollect, in flashes, drenching sweat, searing pain in the chest and back, frantic adult mumblings, the dim light of a bedside lamp, eerie, shifting shadows, my own breathing, hurried and shallow, needing more air, yet fearful of the pain of a deep breath.

Then Dr Tom took command, issuing orders, quietly, with authority. I heard the name 'Ely' mentioned – the nursing home. The pain diminished. I made a journey in the back of the old Vauxhall Fourteen, wrapped in blankets in the back seat.

We trundled down George's Street, along the Main Street, past the station, out the Ferrycarrig road, across the old bridge over the Slaney, past Kaat's Strand, along the tree-lined coast road of Ferrybank. The pain had gone.

We travelled on sedately, through wind-rent clouds; a fitful moon beamed patches of light on the river. And then through the gates of Ely, round the drive under the tall pines, soughing in the night wind, up to the open front door.

Movement in climbing from the car brought sharp flashes of pain again. Everything went hazy after that.

Through the large doors of Ely, whispering nuns in white swishing habits, the chink of long heavy rosary beads swaying from their waists. All sounds echoing faintly in the big corridor.

Then lying in the hospital room, piled with hot rubber jars, sweating heavily. No pain but a terrible lassitude, a dreadful weakness, frightful in its weight, wanting to raise an arm, a hand, and as in a dream, not being able to.

Then the priest, mumbling, the purple surplice, a smell of incense or candle, long, clear and strong. My mother, watching in a kind of wonder.

Then nothing.

RECOVERY

'You can't kill a bad thing, soldier.' Dr Tom McCabe was sitting on the bed, smiling.

The room was bright with morning sun. Outside, a silvered river sparkled. I felt well, still weak but rested. It had been touch and go. Hence the priest. 'But only the good die young,' beamed the doctor. 'You'll be around for a good while yet.'

Tom McCabe was the personification of a family doctor, kind, approachable.

Not knowing that convalescents were meant to be poorly,I began to recover impatiently.But the environment prevailed. I quietened, settled into a pattern, reading voraciously, resting, eating, sleeping.

Over the weeks, I watched the river through all levels of ebb and flood, from the depths of tranquillity to the heights of storm, from bright and dazzling in the daylight to murky sinister shifting in the dark of night.

Like the river, I continued in my own rhythm of resting,

reading, sleeping, eating. And breathing. Doctor Tom showed me that.

At first I'd ignored him, pretending to follow his instructions. Then he hit the right button. He said I could be delicate all my life, would pant going upstairs, never again play a game, could forget about swimming, sailing, football. Or I could help myself. And never get that pain again.

So I listened. I practised what he told me to do and I got better, a lot faster than was expected. I soon got into the habit. Normal breathing, even deep breathing became painless. I learned quickly, practised regularly. Within months I was up and about again, fully recovered.

Over the years I kept doing the breathing exercises, learning and developing new techniques and applications. At various times in life I came across disciplines, such as yoga and martial arts, in which breathing played an essential role. Some of these disciplines gave names to techniques which I had discovered in my own personal practice, in developing the habits I had nurtured since child-hood. The realisation that these were established customs reinforced my belief in and adherence to the routines.

It has been my privilege to have taught many hundreds of people these simple techniques. In many instances, people were interested only in learning these and nothing further, or were capable of doing only these, because of physical disability, or lack of time or some other factor.

Where these routines have been practised faithfully, with a bit of a will, there has always been an improvement in health, wellbeing and vitality. It does of course take an act of faith and hope to do them consistently. The basic system has worked for the thousands who have done so.

So to that idea, and to those people who made that act of faith in themselves and in this method, this book is dedicated.

1

COULD THIS BE FOR YOU?

Stress is ruthless. It doesn't care who it attacks. And when it does hit, the victim is devoured. Every aspect of life is affected.

Stress is a physical reaction. It is not exaggerating to say that it tears people apart, mentally and emotionally.

The problems of modern living bring it about. We live in an age of irony: progress is centred around labour-saving and time-saving. Working habits are becoming geared to leisure, so much that there is now an enormous and growing leisure industry. The irony is that while our standard of living is improving, our quality of life is deteriorating.

Most of the illnesses prevalent today are directly related to our lifestyle. The speed, the tension, the ever-present imperative, the relentless immediacy of living today are taking their toll on our health. We have not yet adapted to the simmering urgency of today's society, where the need to be ready for all eventualities keeps us in a constant state of tension.

Some tension is fine. You need enough to get you out of bed, perform well enough in work and keep yourself focused on your goals. This could be seen as positive stress. It's the other one that gets to you – that becomes *distress*. This is the one that keeps you awake at night, interferes with your digestion, tears your concentration in shreds, blows problems out of proportion, makes your heart race, sunders your relationships, and because you can't seem to do anything about it, develops in you a self-perpetuating feeling of self-loathing, underpinned by a foundation of ever-increasing guilt.

So what can be done? A lot. Stress is a symptom. It is a reaction maybe to fear, anxiety, resentment, worry, guilt – any of the negative emotions which we can experience at any time in our lives. These negative emotions which can have such an effect on you are brought about by any number of circumstances. Some of these circumstances you can change or avoid or overcome; others you can't. So if you can't change the circumstance, try the alternative: alter your reaction to it.

That might mean swallowing your pride, compromising on something about which you feel very strongly, forgiving the unforgivable or taking a stand, accepting the risk and being responsible for it.

This might all sound a bit drastic. A lot of people suffering from stress aren't really that distressed. It's a matter of degree. But whatever the intensity, you either change the things that are distressing you or you change your reaction to them. Or you remain unhappy.

A stress-management technique may not solve your problems but it will help you cope with them. And frequently, that is what is needed for the beginnings of a solution to be discovered.

I put that question to a friend of mine some years ago. He hesitantly agreed with me, mainly because he didn't want to be rude and couldn't think of any real reason to disagree. But he thought that the idea was too simple, too obvious, that if it were that simple everybody would practise the techniques and stress would no longer be a problem in life.

His hesitancy highlighted the two main obstacles to managing stress. The first is that there are techniques which can be learned by anyone. Tranquillity, peace, imperturbability can be learned, just like anything else. It is a skill to learn them. And all skills have their rudiments. Secondly, the skill has to be practised, rehearsed, repeated, released, applied, internalised and integrated into your life so that it is a strong powerful part of your character and personality.

Remember, we practise worry, fear and anxiety and panic all the time. Not consciously; rather we let them into our minds and hearts and allow them to rampage all over our days. Stress management is a reversal of that unconscious acceptance; it is deciding consciously to use the intelligence you've got to reverse the role your mind may have tricked you into playing.

The method is simple but, paradoxically, not easy. You'll find all sorts of excuses not to practise. And practice is vital. No practice – no skill.

If you wanted to play the piano, you'd expect to learn and practise scales, finding where the notes are, what they sound like, how they can vary in tone and meaning whether you pound them or stroke them. The skills in this book are a bit simpler than piano scales. They're accessible any time, all the time, and all you need is the desire to learn them. But most importantly, if you do practise these methods, learn them, use them, bring them into your life, your rewards will be far greater than the trouble you'll have taken to learn them.

You will be amazed at the music you will bring to your own life and the lives of those around you.

2

THE FIRST STEP

Knowing where you're going. That's your very first objective. Think about it. Be clear in your mind what image you've got of yourself, how you want to be, where you want to go. Write it down.

Whether you want to lose weight, improve your nerves, develop powerful concentration, increase your fitness, make yourself lean and muscular, trim flab off tummy, hips, thighs, develop strength, speed, power, improve your game of golf, soccer, rugby, draughts or your performance in business, make yourself more attractive, to others and to yourself – write it down.

See it and then write it down. Articulate it so that there is no doubt in your mind or your heart about it. Write it down so that the words on the paper describe the picture in your mind. Don't ask anyone else whether or not it's OK or whether they think you could or should do it. Just write it down. You're not concerned about anyone's approval or opinion at this stage. This is a decision about something in your life that is no one else's business.

That's your first step; knowing where you're going. Once you have done this, you have something to aim for, a goal. If you don't have a goal, an aim which you will take the necessary steps to get to, you've just got a wish.

A wish is something you dream about, in a woolly irresolute kind of way, like wishing for six numbers in the Lotto, wishing you were on some sunny beach or in deep and tranquil countryside. We all do that at times. Most of us do it a lot. On Monday we wish it was Friday and on Friday we wish we had more money. We tend to wish for different things without doing anything about getting them.

Goals change all that. And you can start anywhere, at any time in the day or night or at any age. When you've got a goal, a real and achievable aim in your life, the empty wishing stops and the real living starts. You become one of those people about whom it's said: 'S/he knows where s/he's going.' And once you know what you want, where you want to go, there are three factors to get you there:

- Knowing what to do
- Knowing how to do it
- Getting on with it

This principle applies to anything.

STAGES

Every endeavour must be taken in stages. There are learning stages, stepping stages, new development stages. By the time you're at the slightly higher stages in this course, you'll already be a different person. You will then integrate your own development systematically into your life. The growth is comfortable, simple and natural.

The simplicity of the plan lies in the basic steps. They're all you need to keep developing. As you practise them, you will already have started on your journey. All you have to do is keep taking the steps. At your own pace. Don't hurry.

Keep doing them. Let it happen. You will travel comfortably, inevitably. As you reach different stages you will find that your view of the journey alters. Your health will improve and you will be getting exactly where you want to go, just as you would in a journey where you intend to walk from A to Z. You will go through all the points A, B and C and so on till you get to the end. What gets you there is the simple fact of taking the first step, then the second. Then you keep putting one foot in front of the other.

The first stage is laying the foundation:

This is the development of the basic necessities that make the rest possible. All the skills and abilities you develop in the future will depend for their effectiveness on the knowing, the understanding and the practice of these rudiments.

Read that again. Absorb it. You are going to learn skills and you will become so familiar with the rudiments of these skills that you won't need to think about them. Just as you walk, close your fingers around an object to lift it, open them to drop it, put food in your mouth, lie, sit, stand or any of the other countless things we do automatically during our lives.

The things you're going to do are very simple. In fact you've been doing them all your life so far. All you'll need to do now is get better at them, think about how you've been doing them and how you'll need to do them to get them working for you. Over the years I have seen thousands of people, of all ages, improve their health and their lives simply and effectively by constant application of these simple steps. If you take them, you will greatly enhance the value of everything else you do. If you neglect them, no matter how hard you work, you will diminish, considerably, the worth of your efforts.

To learn to use your posture is simple.

Remember the three factors involved in reaching your goals:

- Knowing what to do
- Knowing how to do it
- Getting on with it

So let's look at the first thing that needs to be done.

While the sketch on the opposite page may seem to be a bit dramatic, you should think again before you dismiss it. For a start, if you carry yourself even slightly like this, remember that it goes on all day long. After a while, the skeletal muscles which were meant to be holding you upright adapt to this position: they become contorted to accommodate the incorrect posture. There's also a huge and constant strain on the tendons attaching them to the bones. And the ligaments that attach bone to bone are also strained into the wrong position. This affects the joints, which are meant to be points of movement but now become dislocated in an effort to hold the body upright.

All you need now is to carry a few shopping bags or a bucket of coal, pick up a child, reach into a cupboard, swing a hammer, haul a lawnmower, and there's a very good chance that eventually a shoulder, an elbow, a knee, a hip, some part of your back is going to give. A muscle pulls, a disc pops, a tendon strains or a ligament tears.

Even if this doesn't happen, your body has come to accept this posture, adapting in its own way, so that when you do stand straight, your body, conditioned to wrong positions, will feel uncomfortable as if you're out of alignment when you're not.

There are other effects too. Because your chest is

POOR POSTURE

- CURVED SPINE
- CONGESTED ORGANS
- CONGESTED LUNGS
- SHALLOW BREATHING
- POOR CIRCULATION
- INDIGESTION
- ROUNDED SHOULDERS
- TENSION
- DISEASE

concave, and your stomach muscles are out of tone, your breathing will be shallow. Less air in your lungs means less oxygen in your blood, less vitality, poorer concentration, poorer muscle tone. More of this vital function later. And the peristaltic action of your stomach muscles will be diminished, so your intestines will not effectively excrete the waste matter from your system and you will be inducing the source of auto-poisoning of our inactive society: constipation.

The main organs, heart, liver, kidney, brain, cannot function efficiently. Your resistance to colds, flu, fatigue is lowered. You get tired, run-down, out of sorts. In short you are not well. You're not sick but you're not well. Many people think that if they're not sick, they must be well. This is not necessarily so. People function at half their capacity, mentally, physically and emotionally, because they're not as well as they could be.

Let's look at the figure again.

Go to a wall. Put your back to it. Let your head, shoulder blades, buttocks, calves and heels either touch the wall on all points, or come as close to it as possible, without forcing the issue. Relax. Stand straight but loose. Feel yourself touching the wall at all these points. Let yourself ease into the wall, so you feel at ease but straight. These are the key words:

Straight but at ease.

Let yourself settle into the wall. Move your shoulders up and down. Loll your head from side to side. Move your hips and shift your calves and heels against the wall. Be aware of all points touching.

Stay at ease. Let your arms hang loose at the sides, wrists loose and hands dangling. Be loose. Stay loose. Be aware of your body weight travelling down your skeleton and meeting the ground squarely on your heels and the entire foot. Feel the weight evenly distributed between each foot. Have your knees straight, hips and pelvis level; keep your back straight but not rigid.

Be at ease. Imagine a plumb-line going directly from your head, down through the centre point between your shoulders, down along the back and through the pelvis and cutting directly down between your knees and ankles, so your legs are comfortably straight and your feet equidistant from the line, your body weight carrying evenly down each leg and on to each foot.

Feel that position. Be aware of each point and of the stance as a whole. Now, gently holding everything in place, step from the wall. Stand with everything as it was when you were at the wall. Feel the ease and correctness of each position as you hold it, gently but firmly, in place. Let yourself stand like this for a while. Experience the straightness, the balance, the evenness of your stance.

It may feel awkward at first. Do not be alarmed if this is the case. Most people feel as if they're rigidly out of alignment. This is because, having become accustomed to being in the incorrect posture, they now feel *this* to be the wrong one.

When you've stood like this for a short while, go back to the wall and check your alignments again. You may find you've more readjusting to do because even in the couple of minutes you've been free-standing, your posture may have reverted to some or all aspects to which it had become accustomed.

HOW TO CURE YOURSELF OF FATIGUE

Posture is the basis of all fitness benefits. If your limbs, muscles, tendons and ligaments are not being used in their natural positions, they try to use themselves unnaturally. This is difficult. It is also dangerous.

The first thing a trained posture will bring you is ease. With one muscle helping another and each one working individually as it should, the balance of the whole is in harmony. This helps your body to function efficiently from day to day, hour to hour, minute to minute. In this environment, the lungs, heart, diaphragm, circulation, all find their balance. The heartbeat, breath, digestion, elimination, glandular secretion, are all more likely to work in the way nature intended.

If our posture is incorrect, we can't use our lungs fully. The circulation will be impaired, diminishing the value of any exercise. Good posture helps the lungs and also the stomach muscles. This promotes a kneading of the main organs and helps the circulation, carrying in fresh oxygen, getting rid of wastes. Its peristaltic effect on the intestines and the large bowel in particular helps regularity.

Posture is a vital factor in health and wellbeing. When your posture is adequate, everything you do, from climbing a stairs to running for a bus, has an effect on the abdominal muscles and on the whole area of the bowel.

When the posture is right, all the major muscles work more efficiently. The blood is pushed along the veins, revitalising the circulation. Poor circulation is the greatest known cause of fatigue. When circulation is recharged, which simply means that the blood is surging around the body as it was meant to, the muscles, organs, brain and nerve cells all benefit. When you correct your posture you will notice an increase in your own vitality. This is no

GOOD POSTURE

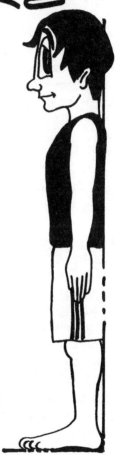

- COMFORT
- EFFICIENT BREATHING
- EASE
- VITALITY
- GOOD CIRCULATION
- SOUND DIGESTIVE SYSTEM
- ATTITUDE
- CONFIDENCE
- OPTIMISM
- HEALTH

psychosomatic reaction. This is purely physical. And it is permanent. Indeed it is often more effective than taking up an exercise programme.

If all you do is correct your posture, and put more vigour into your daily activities, you will get the benefit of basic fitness and vitality. And while your physical activity may be less than the person who runs, jogs, dances or trains with weights, the constancy and continuity of the benefit of you receive will ensure overall fitness.

In other words, the minute-by-minute fitness value of your regime may be less, but consistent positive exertion has a cumulative effect.

You'll be surprised at how quickly your body responds to a bit of good treatment. The movement and the response settle into a routine. The better the movement, the more efficient the response. The more efficient the response, the better the body parts and organs can make the movement.

Developing the habit of good posture lays the foundation. But you have to do it. All the time. Give it priority. In a short time, a very short time, it becomes natural. And then you are ready to take the next step to healthy living and enhanced wellbeing.

In the meantime, keep your posture right. Keep it comfortable. Keep it at ease. But keep it. For once and forever. It is the key to your next step.

One final point on the simplicity of these techniques. You may read this and think it's too simple to be true. If it was so good, everyone would be telling you about it. Everyone did tell you about it, at one time or another. Just as everyone told everyone who told you. It got beaten to death as something to be done but it was never properly explained why you should do it. Now you know why.

So do it. Don't wonder whether it will work or how long

it's going to take or how you'll look or if anyone will notice how you stand, walk, fit more stylishly into your suit.

Just do it. And enjoy it. And then do it again. And keep on doing it.

It works.

STAND UP FOR YOURSELF!

How do you stand? How do you sit? How do you move when you walk?

We've all been told at some time or other: 'Put your shoulders back!', 'Don't slouch!', Walk straight!', 'Sit up straight!'. And not without good reason. The trouble is that it was always just an order levelled at us, so that as soon as the order-giver was out of sight, the shoulders slouched again, the chest caved in and the stomach sagged.

Pity. Because if we'd paid some attention, straightened our shoulders, held ourselves erect, comfortably, not at rigid attention, and got into that habit instead of the other one, we'd have laid the foundation for fitness, vitality and energy. Not only would we feel better physically but better mentally too. When you walk straight, ca
rry yourself as nature intended, you have presence in your own mind and you also afford the brain and nerve cells the oxygen they need for efficiency.

That's not overstating the case.

3

THE SECOND SIMPLE STEP

Now that you've got the concept of steps, taken the first and seen the significance of it, you're ready for the next.

You're probably wondering when you're going to have to heave, grunt, push and strain your way to wellbeing and fitness. That's what most people imagine when they think of getting fit. And of course exercise, at all its levels, does have a place in fitness.

But wait a minute! Why do people exercise? Why do doctors recommend activity, a jog or a walk or workout in the gym? Is it because it makes you sweat? Or because it makes your muscles pump? Or because it makes the blood surge around your body and tones up your heart?

Yes, it does all these things – and what wonderful things they are – to keep the body well and in good working order. But exercise does something more basic and profound than these things: it makes you pant, breathe more deeply and quickly so that your body becomes drenched in oxygen from the air you breathe.

This is your main physiological benefit – improved breathing. And that's why your doctor wants you to be active. He wants your lungs to work at their optimum capacity. Then, and only then, can the cells of every part of your body benefit. The air you breathe goes into your lungs. The oxygen is collected from the air by the billions of blood cells passing through the lungs. This oxygenated blood is then passed through the heart, which is a muscular pump, and sent around the body. As it circulates, the oxygen in the blood cells burns up the wastes and toxins in your system and converts them into carbon dioxide. This carbon dioxide is then delivered back to the lungs, from where you exhale it. Your next in-breath takes up more fresh air, the circulating blood cells take up the oxygen from this clean air and off they go again to do the same job, all over again.

As the build-up of toxins and wastes is fairly constant, we need a lot of oxygen to keep our bodies from becoming congested. This is why exercise is so good for you. When you train, you pant and puff and flood your body with oxygen, cleanse the system and flush out a lot of waste. This process affects every part of our bodies: the muscles, organs, nervous system, brain cells, bones and even the skin.

Millions of people have noticed, within weeks of a light exercise programme, how their skin has cleared, their eyes too. Their senses become sharper as their bodies become leaner.

The largest contributory factor in this metamorphosis is the increase in supply of oxygen to the body. It follows that if the most important product of any training programme is oxygen, the most important activity in our lives is breathing.

Most of the time our posture is poor, our breathing is shallow and our circulation stumbling halfheartedly around our bodies. The cells that make up our muscles, bones, nerves and brains are supplied with just about enough oxygen for us to struggle along from day to day.

It's small wonder we get tired, can't concentrate, feel

29

nervy, irritable, out of sorts. We need more oxygen. We need to breathe better, to activate our systems, open the lungs, breathe deeply, regularly, walk straight, carry ourselves so that our lungs, muscles, bones and joints can all move, breathe and live the way nature intended.

This can be achieved very simply. You've already got the first part, the posture. Now you're going to get posture and breathing working for you.

THE POWER OF THE IMAGINATION

Think of your lungs as a pear-shaped device. The greatest volume is at the lower part. Look at the sketch

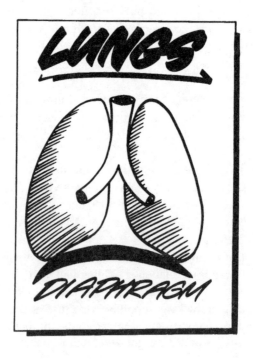

THE LUNGS

If you're running after a bus or running from an angry dog, you'll go flat out and your lungs will function naturally and forcefully to give you as much oxygen as possible. The rib-cage that surrounds your lungs and your diaphragm, that floor of muscle under the lungs, all contrive to work in such a way that the fullest possible capacity of your lungs is in operation.

On the other hand if someone tells you to take a deep breath, you'll most likely push out the chest, push in the stomach, pull back your shoulders. And you'll be only half-filling the lungs.

So what you'll have to do is this:

- Arrange your posture as shown previously
- Let your stomach muscles flop out and relax

With your stomach muscles relaxed, distended, breathe in gently through the nose. Keep the stomach muscles out.

- Air in
- Stomach out
- As you keep breathing in, the chest areas of your lungs will begin to fill. Your rib-cage will rise and your stomach muscles will begin to come in anyway.

- Air going in
- Rib-cage rising
- Stomach levelling, beginning to come in

As you keep on breathing in, the shoulders finally rise, the chest area expands and your stomach muscle flattens.

Your lungs are now full.

Once your lungs are comfortably filled with air, let the air whoosh out through your mouth, making sure you are standing straight.

Use your imagination. Think of your stomach muscles as a corset, tightening in on the lower part of your lungs, squeezing in the bottom of the pear-shape, shoving all the stale air from your lungs. Keep standing straight. Breathe out steadily, gently, till there is no air left to come.

- Air going out
- Stomach going in

Now when your lungs are *completely* empty, seal your nose and mouth and let no air back in for a moment. Then, opening your nasal passages, let the air drift back in through your nose, your stomach muscles flopping out as before.

Repeat the sequence, filling the stomach area, chest area, shoulder area. Then whoosh the air out gently but forcefully through the mouth, till there's no air left to come. Hold the air out for a count of three with your stomach muscles tensed in. Then *relax* the stomach muscles muscles again, opening your nasal passages and letting the air drift in as before.

It's a skill. It takes practice.Call one complete inhalation and exhalation a round of breath. Paying attention to keeping the posture right, and not forcing anything, put the sequence into operation as shown. Do five full rounds of breath at a time.

At this stage, don't do more than five rounds at a time. If you find it difficult to do more than two or three correctly, don't worry. This is a new skill and it takes practice. What's important is to get it right. Once you have that, you can do as many or as few as suits your programme. You'll be doing it right and getting benefit from every breath you take.

THE REASONS WHY

The main reason for doing this is that it will make you ready to start doing what will help you get fitter, feel better and get more out of your life. And these benefits start coming to you as soon as you start the practice. For a start, you're going to increase the amount of air going into your lungs. Not only that, you're doing the very thing that will train your lungs to work for you all the time.

Did you know that the average breath of the average man is about 500 cc (half a litre)? And that our lungs are capable of taking in up to four litres of air? That happens when we take a complete breath. If your lungs and the muscles and breathing apparatus surrounding them are trained, your capacity to breathe more deeply and effectively increases immediately. If you only increase your breathing by another half-litre, you're straight away increasing your breathing efficiency by 100 per cent.

This means more oxygen in your system. Oxygen is the ingredient that gives you life-force. Every part of your body benefits: your blood, muscle, brain cells, nervous system. It's hardly a wonder that you feel better when you start your programme.

FEELING BETTER

This is a curious phenomenon. Over the years, I've seen many people start a simple, effective breathing programme and when they applied themselves with a bit of will they invariably reported a terrific improvement in how they felt. A lot of them suspected that the psychological effect of the practice of breathing was having a beneficial psychosomatic effect on them. That's a perfectly reasonable thing to suppose. But the effect is physical. The body responds readily to any assistance you give it in re-establishing itself as a healthy, strong, vibrant unit.

Remember, the main reason people feel the benefits of exercising, whether they do aerobics, weight-training, dancing or sports, is that it makes them breathe efficiently. So it would be difficult not to feel better after a good breathing programme.

By doing the following breathing exercises, you'll learn how to get the main benefit of exercise, without sweat, inconvenience or expenditure of time. Nice thought, isn't it?

When you take that little bit of trouble to correct your posture and deepen your breathing, you'll also be training your system to work for you all the time. Your trained lungs will have an enhancing effect on every activity. This in turn will increase the ease with which you perform your daily activities, which in turn will greatly increase your fitness and sense of wellbeing. And of course this will strengthen your posture, improve your breathing, tone the muscles, help you sleep, relax the system. So what you're doing at this stage is instigating a basic but effective manoeuvre that will be the beginning of a self-perpetuating beneficial cycle.

After a short while, as your technique improves, and with it your fitness and health, the benefits tend to accumulate at a rate which most people quite simply find amazing. You may wonder what the secret is. Wonder on. There is no secret. If you do the simple things, do them well and often, the results will take care of themselves.

HOW TO GET THE BEST
FROM YOUR PROGRAMME

When you start doing your programme, you may have a tendency to check how you feel for results. Instead, commit yourself to the process.

Remember that every breathing session is an event in itself but it's the accumulated result of the process, on a day-to-day basis, that you're aiming for. So don't worry whether you're getting fitter or better. Don't annoy yourself by wondering whether or not it's working. Do it. It will work.

WHAT TO DO

The first thing you do is assume the posture which will allow you to perform your breathing exercise. This can be done standing or sitting, straight and at ease (a kitchen chair will do). With your mouth closed, tongue resting gently against your lower teeth, begin to breathe in slowly through your nose. Let the air drift in. Slowly. Let your stomach relax. Feel the air easing down through your nose, through your windpipe and into the bottom part of your lungs. Keep it coming evenly. See in your mind's eye the lungs filling at the lower part. See your rib-cage lifting as the lungs fill. Now see and feel the final draught of air filling the upper part of your lungs.

Without pausing, open the mouth in an 'O' and let the air drift out evenly. See the stomach muscles tightening, the rib-cage contracting and the final instalment of stale air leaving your lungs.

Do this round three or four times, just to get the feel of it, to practise the smoothness of your inhalation and expiration and to develop awareness of the gentle loosening of the stomach muscles as you breathe in and the gentle even tightening as you breathe out.

You will also become aware of the completeness of your breath as you focus your concentration on this simple health-giving activity.

Spend a few minutes doing this, doing five full breaths at a time, relaxing and breathing normally between the breathing rounds

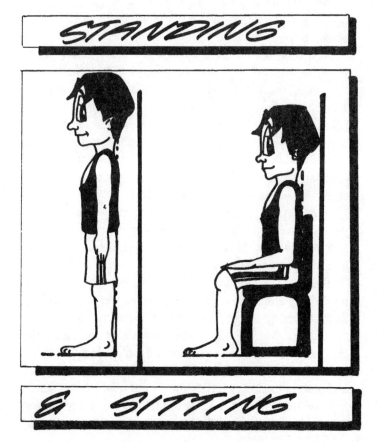

STANDING

& SITTING

CONTROL AND RHYTHM

Developing a good breathing practice requires focus on the breathing and how you're doing it. It is as much a mental as a physical exercise. To breathe well you need to bring rhythm into your practice. Everything in life has a rhythm. We speak in rhythm, we work in rhythm, we exist in a rhythm which pervades the universe and our own world. As the tide flows and ebbs, as night follows day, as spring follows winter, so we are subject to our own internal rhythms. Breathing is the very rhythm of life and it can be enhanced and developed.

You'll need a watch or a clock to do this. Standing, or sitting, as shown, start breathing in, as taught. Starting at a count of one, breathe in over five seconds. Pay attention. This means you start to breathe in at one and complete your in-breath when you get to five. Be precise. Have your lungs full by the time you get to the fifth second. Not the fourth, not the sixth. Fill your lungs at the fifth second precisely. This means you have to time your breathing to coincide with the count of five seconds.

Now, opening your mouth in the 'O' shape, you push in your stomach muscles and let the air push out in an even and forceful breath, again over five seconds, so that your lungs empty completely.

Precision is important. You must make sure to have the lungs fully empty by the time you get to the count of five. Don't speed up the count or slow it down to coincide with the pace of your breath. Make your breath coincide with the count – both on the in-breath and the out-breath. Empty the lungs completely. Let the stomach muscles contract and push in the lungs, letting the air out freely and evenly. Practise this timing for a few rounds, so you get a feel for the rhythm of the breath. Do three consecutive rounds.

That will take you just thirty seconds – breathing in on five, out on five on each round. You will find that by the time you've completed the third breath, to this rhythm, you will become proficient, and all the muscles and organs involved will be working in unison to help you achieve your aim.

Now we're going to take the process a step further. This time after you've inhaled and then exhaled, *hold your breath* out. That's right, hold it *out*. This will let the residual carbon dioxide, wastes and toxins, drift out from your system. Also, as you hold the breath out, a vacuum forms in the lungs. When you open your air passages again, after holding your breath out for five seconds, this vacuum sucks the air back down into your lungs, opening them naturally and easily and filling every cubic centimetre of them. In other words, you will be taking a complete breath rather than just a deep one.

You will then be using your lungs naturally and fully, and you'll find also that your stomach muscles will distend and contract more effectively through their full range of movement, giving all the internal organs a good toning.

Your sequence is now as follows:

- Breathe in over a count of five seconds.
- Breathe out over a count of five seconds.
- Hold your breath out over a count of five seconds.

That makes fifteen seconds in all.

Practise a few sequences to get the feel of the rhythm and the sense of control. Now, sticking strictly to the rhythm in the completion of the round, do two full consecutive rounds. This will take thirty seconds.

When you can take two breaths at precisely the time on the clock, in for five, out for five, holding out for five, do four consecutive breaths. This takes one minute and in that minute you'll be helping to cleanse your system, enliven your circulation, feed much-needed oxygen to the brain and nerves and tone up your stomach muscles.

When you have mastered the tempo precisely as instructed, you can work the entire sequence, maintaining smoothness and rhythm, for up to ten breaths. That's 150 seconds or two-and-a half minutes. Find this time in a place where you can concentrate totally on your breathing with no fear of interruption. Be ruthless with yourself in doing it. You'll find all sorts of excuses to get out of it. Give yourself some time. Find this bit of space in your day. You owe it to yourself and to others. You'll feel better for it. Your day will be calmer and more invigorated.

Find at least four spots in your day when you can do this without interruption. Make them your spots of solitude, when you find time to be with yourself. This will give you time to stop in your day and check with yourself how you're getting on, to see if you're going where you want, to breathe, to keep the day and its events in perspective.

Frequently this is all you will need to get back on track and take the stress and tension out of life. If you do this two-and-a-half minute cycle four times a day, that's a total of ten minutes. You'll need a minute to set yourself up and focus your attention on the exercise. But it's still not much more than ten minutes a day and that leaves you twenty-three hours and fifty minutes to get on with your life.

Can you afford those ten minutes? Can you afford not to afford them? The benefits, mentally and physically, are totally out of proportion to the little bit of trouble it takes.

NATURAL MEDITATION

There is a strong meditative value in the system. To keep your concentration solely on what you are doing for the ten breaths may not be as easy as it sounds.

There are thousands of ideas, thoughts, reactions, impressions, memories running through your mind every minute. This is one of the causes of stress. The mind can become restless and unfocused, leading to a sense of confusion and anxiety.

Your breathing exercises, conscientiously done, will help you to still the mind and calm the emotions. Done regularly, they will help to bring a sense of ease and perspective into your life, taking the panic out of potentially harmful reactions, bringing a feeling of control and purpose. After a while you will begin to look forward to doing them.

When you're starting, if you find your mind wandering, bring it back gently but positively to where it should be focusing. At first you may have many distractions. But perseverance and practice will help you to overcome this problem and you will soon be able to focus your thoughts unwaveringly.

This skill overflows into all the other parts of your life. As you develop the faculty of concentration, or rediscover it, you will find the quality of your life improving in all sorts of ways. For interest and variation, there are other rhythms to practise, but do these only when you are completely familiar with the 5-5-5 rhythm.

Try the following when you are particularly tense and wound-up. It will really concentrate the mind and calm the nerves. Again, using your watch or clock, breathe in for a count of seven seconds. Smoothly and without pause, draw the air in through your nose and at the top of the breath, without pausing, let the air come out through the formed

'O' of your mouth. Breathe out evenly and smoothly for a count of eight seconds, emptying the lungs precisely on the count of eight. Contracting the stomach, firmly but gently, hold the lungs empty for a count of five seconds.

Practise this till you can do three consecutive breaths, precisely timed: breathing in for a count of seven seconds, breathing out for a count of eight seconds, holding out for a count of five seconds. This will take one minute.

When you can do this easily, you are now ready, physically and mentally, for a more advanced breathing technique which will greatly enhance your physical ability to use your lungs and will also tone up your body. It will improve your concentration by demanding fidelity to the precision with which you do it.

ADVANCED BREATHING

Sit or stand quietly. Breathe in gently but fully over seven seconds. Breathe out fully over eight seconds. Hold out for fifteen seconds.

On the second breath, control the tendency to let the air rush into your lungs – unless you're experiencing discomfort. Otherwise, let the air drift in over the seven seconds again, out over the eight, and hold out again for the fifteen.

Do only the two breaths at a time but do them with accuracy and precise timing, paying attention to your posture, making sure it's maintained throughout the round, using your stomach muscles and rib-cage and shoulders as shown, and of course keeping the completion of the in-breath and the out-breath and holding out strictly in time to the count of the second hand on your watch or clock.

DYNAMIC BREATHING

Now that a fundamental technique has been established, it is as good a time as any to analyse what you're doing. This will further the meditative quality of your work.

You are now developing a conscious use of the breathing apparatus. The lungs, the rib-cage, the stomach muscles and diaphragm are all consciously used to effect the maximum inhalation and exhalation. Do not fall into the trap of being blinded by numbers at this stage. Many people, at all levels of fitness, become fixed on the number of times something is done. This is as true for weight-lifters as it is for martial artists as it is for yoga students. What is vital now is to learn and put into practice the technique which will allow optimum working of your breathing equipment.

This means working on *how* you do the exercises. But don't get into the habit of just going through the motions, filling up the quota for the day.

Even should you do less, do better. Use your imagination. Take a moment or two to consider what you are doing: using the various parts of your body to maximise your feeling of health. Make every breath the perfect round. This concentration will help you to use the mind as well as your body and it will enhance enormously the value of every studied breath.

While you are doing one round of breathing, focus your mind on every split second of every phase of the breath – the beginning of the inhalation, the evenness of the breath, the filling of the lungs from the bottom up, the completion of breathing in and the smoothness with which you move to the exhalation, the steadiness of the out-flow and the tensing in of the stomach muscles as you empty the lungs completely and then hold them empty, still sitting or standing erect but at ease, the only discernible tension being on the tautened abdominal muscles.

Then when the breath is fully finished, bring your mind on to the next breath, think your way through it again, make it as near perfect a breath as you can. There really is quite a lot to think about. What you are doing is a long way from just taking air in and blowing it out. It is the thought behind it that gives it the real depth of benefit, the mental application that makes the difference to the physical development and the mental relaxation.

You will also pay attention to your posture throughout the rounds of breath. You have to stay erect but at ease, loose enough to allow the elasticity of your body to work while not being so loose as to slouch. All this takes thought. None of your breathing will have maximum effect if you don't constantly monitor how you're holding yourself.

So:

- Concentrate
- Focus on every breath, for every second

BREATHING AND ATTITUDE

Our breathing, rhythms, depths and shallows, are all very finely tuned to our minute-to-minute living. How we are feeling, what we're thinking, how we are reacting to the experiences of the day are all reflected in our breathing. As our circumstances change from hour to hour, our breathing patterns change accordingly.

You don't need a medical degree to grasp this. We've all experienced a quickening of the breath at some point: when we're given a piece of particular news or we're in a tense situation. You're likely also to have noticed how calm and rhythmic your breathing is when you're relaxed and content. And of course we've all experienced the sigh of relief and savoured the immense satisfaction that comes with it, when the tension of anxiety has loosened its grip and our lungs open up, drawing the much-needed air into the depths.

Just as circumstances affect our emotions and may impose an uncomfortable pattern on our breathing, it is also true that we can exert a degree of control on our reactions to circumstances by paying attention to our breathing. While this may not immediately affect the circumstances, it does help to change our reaction and therefore our attitude to them. Research has shown that attitude is frequently more important than the circumstances with which we may be faced.

We have all experienced how, in the space of a short time, a change of attitude can help us to deal with a difficulty in our lives. Sometimes when faced with an unpalatable fact, we may be too shocked or frightened to do anything about it. But often, after an hour, a day, a week or even a night's sleep, the fact doesn't seem so horrific. After a bit more thought, it seems less daunting still, and by the time we sit down and write out a couple of alternative approaches to it, a solution may well have appeared. Time, by itself, allowed our attitude to change.

In modern-day living a lot of little fears accumulate during the day. On their own, they may appear relatively insignificant. Yet the individual fears of missing the bus, being late, dealing with the brown envelope in the hallway, getting caught in the rain, missing the lift, not getting the morning's quota of work finished, not getting on with the boss or a particular colleague, all add up to a general feeling of apprehension. To compound the problem, small and difficult-to-identify fears may be overlooked and not dealt with. These accumulate, to establish a vague but real feeling of unease and uncertainty.

Often, it's these rather than major problems that get us down. The latter can generally be seen, faced and dealt with. The use of any technique that focuses our imagination on a positive activity, constantly, gently, creatively, will tend to dispel the imaginary fears and leave us free to cope with what might well be the real problems in life.

This is the effect of regulating our breathing patterns. The method, once adopted and practised, focuses the mind, stills it and prevents the nerves from creating havoc in our lives. While this technique does not pretend to solve any problem in itself, it will enable you to view it more objectively.

THE VALUE OF BREATHING

Up to a few years ago, breathing exercises were looked on as a kind of esoteric activity, confined to fitness fanatics or practitioners of yoga. Now they have become more appealing to people in sports, business, showbusiness and every walk of life, who use them to improve their performance, increase stamina or simply to help them get through the day.

Taking a couple of minutes to breathe deeply and relax the body recharges the system and refreshes you when energy flags and interest wanes. Concentration spans vary from person to person. Taking a few deep breaths without making a complete break from the activity in hand will help to keep you focused on the work you are doing.

ONE FINAL POINT

Most of us do not breathe nearly well enough to maintain a healthy vitality. The main reason is that our breathing, as we have seen earlier, tends to adapt to our daily needs. Consequently we get into the habit of shallow, ineffectual breathing. The dysfunction persists because the minimum we have to do is to breathe well enough to get us through each day, in other words, just well enough to meet our inactive needs.

This has a debilitating effect, which establishes and perpetuates a vicious circle. As the breathing goes more shallow, the muscles and circulation are starved of oxygen. The body demands less so the lungs give it less. The less it gets, the less it demands; the less the demand, the less is given. Eventually the breathing becomes so shallow as to be a danger to health.

Not only are muscles and blood deprived of necessary oxygen; so are heart, liver, kidney, brain and nerve cells. Activity becomes difficult, nerves are on edge, thinking becomes disjointed, sleep suffers, the digestive system reacts because there is not enough oxygen to transmute the nutrients of our food into healthy body tissue.

A studied and systematic breathing programme will help to restore health, vitalise the system, relax the nerves and generate a form of constructive activity within the main cells. This simple practice will put the mind in a positive frame, help the nerves and muscles and blood feed themselves and the rest of the body and form the basis of sound habits and a healthy life. Thousands have experienced this before.

The trick is just to do it. The success of any undertaking is largely dependent on the belief and attitude adopted by the person at the outset. So do it.

Not too long ago, a friend of mine was facing a serious problem. His personal world had fallen apart and his professional life wasn't much better. The bank was chasing him for cash, the sheriff had called to his premises to repossess some stock in lieu of payment of a civil bill and his right-hand man had left to set up in competition, taking some long-standing profitable clients with him.

We'll call my friend Peter. Now Peter was a resilient man. He got to work early, left late and generally applied himself. So he worked hard and, more importantly, he worked well. He blamed no one for his current circumstances. Even if a situation was apparently not in his favour, he was not one to whine or moan about it. He confronted the problem and tried to see what he could do to set it right. At the time I met him he was under severe and incessant strain. He and his wife had separated acrimoniously, and few things debilitate the mind and body more than animosity and emotional conflict. Personally and professionally, this was a complete reversal of how his life had seemed two years previously.

For some months he racked his brains, searched and prayed, pushed himself to the farther reaches of his imagination, searching for a way through his problems. He believed that such a way could be found. He was not a defeatist but quietly determined. There was, he thought, a way for his business to recover and for his wife and himself to resolve their differences.

Peter and I met a few times when he was in the throes of his crisis. He had always shown a belief in what he perceived our system of breathing and relaxation could do. But like a lot of people, he did not do anything about it till a crisis arose and the system was needed. He saw very clearly the physical and mental effects the circumstances were having on him. He knew that being more relaxed and composed would not change the circumstances outside his control. But he saw how it could alter the aspects over which he could exert control. So he decided to do it.

Not just try it. Not just give it a whirl and hope something good might happen. He instigated a programme to mend his life. Combining a set of breathing techniques and calm meditative relaxation practices, he gradually wound himself down, gently, persistently, positively.

The initial improvement was in his reaction to the prevailing circumstances. The dreadful physical discomforts which usually accompany acute emotional turmoil abated. Aching neck, stiff shoulders, headaches, biliousness, all eased. He felt more calm during the day, more relaxed at evening. Sleep, nature's own restorative agent, improved. Peter's frayed nerves quietened and allowed his improved sleep serve him even better. He paid attention to his diet, not doing anything drastic, but putting into action some simple principles which made his food work for him rather than against him. His whole system began to function in an active and progressive way.

Within a very short time, he was viewing his circumstances objectively, with a strong slant in the positive direction. His worn mind, now rested, began to focus more effectively. He realised that it was time for change in his life. But he knew that he had to bring it about himself. At first it was a change he did not want to contemplate because it represented failure. It appeared to him that he had achieved all he had sought but failed to hold it together.

He reassessed himself, redefined his terms of existence and his aims. He fully recognised culpability in matters in which he believed he'd been his own worst enemy and accepted his losses.

It was simple. Not easy. But simple. But the important thing was that he'd decided.

He started over and now lives a constructive life of hope and effort, dreams and ambitions, free of the baggage that an upset in life can bring. Peter may have failed, but he did not succumb to the seduction of being a loser and this was his strength.

I'm not saying that breathing and relaxing were his saviours in that crisis. He does, though. He breathed. He relaxed. He prayed. He accepted help from wherever it came. And he obviously had the character to see himself through it and remain unembittered and with a kindness in his heart for others. No small feat.

Peter's practices didn't change his circumstances but helped him to maintain a positive outlook, so that when the worst was over and he was left with the bits, he didn't sink under a tide of self-pity but took a breath, kicked free of the wreckage and struck out for where he wanted to go. He was afloat, buoyant, intact.

That's a pretty extreme example of how even under very adverse circumstances, one can keep one's sense of worth and hope. It doesn't have to be that bad before you decide you can benefit from a little self-help. So start on your own programme now. No matter what your own circumstances are, be assured that your programme will help.

Maybe a little. Perhaps a lot.

You'll know when you do it.

4

EXERCISE AND EXERCISES

Exercise has several aims. The first is to train the heart, which is only a muscle and like any muscle, responds readily to light and regular training. It will function more efficiently and do more work, with less effort. This is how exercise helps the heart.

The important thing is to train it and not strain it. The overall effect you're looking for is a stronger, more robust and more efficient heart muscle. This is what gives you better circulation. That means you'll have more vitality, be warmer in cold weather, have increased resistance to colds and fatigue, and be able to relax, concentrate and eliminate toxins from your system with efficiency. Not bad for a start, is it?

The second thing you will get from light regular exercise is an improved capacity to process more oxygen into the blood from the air you breathe. This comes about because of the heavier, more complete, breathing you'll have to do during the exercise. The deeper breathing you'll be doing, or if you prefer, the light panting, will mean that more air is being sucked into the lungs and that the oxygen from this air is being circulated through your body by your fitter heart. This extra oxygen will combust, or burn up, the wastes and toxins in your system and expel them as carbon dioxide in your breath. That means your system will be cleaner, clearer and purer, free from the burden of poisons and able to get on with the job it was meant to do: build healthy tissue and maintain your system in good working order.

Incidentally, don't think you've got to train to breathlessness in order to get fit. All you need is to get yourself moving sufficiently (you'll soon see how easy this is) to get yourself breathing a bit more heavily than normal. Then the various exercises, simple and enjoyable as they are, done with comfort and regularity, will get you the results you're looking for.

Breathing more fully to open the lungs and training your heart as a muscle are the basis of fitness. You're better off keeping exercise light and enjoyable. That way you'll stay at it and get a lasting benefit in every aspect of your life. Don't make the mistake that some people do, going too hard and too fast. Even if they are able for it, after a while it becomes a chore and loses its appeal. They become bored and disillusioned. They stop. They're back at the start, only worse off. They have disappointment and reluctance to overcome before they start again.

Your individual workout, especially at the start, may be of a lesser fitness value in itself but if you practise it regularly the cumulative effect will be far superior and will be with you always, enhancing your daily living long after the cult follower has dropped off and lost his few hard-gained benefits.

The first few exercises you will need to do are gentle stretches and warm-ups. These are to get the blood circulating, the lungs and the heart working, and the joints and the muscles ready for your session. Relax and enjoy them. Don't worry about whether you're using the right style or if you've got the figure that you want right now.

These will come. Just do what you feel you can, in comfort, without placing any strain anywhere.

Getting used to doing exercises is a bit like swimming or playing a musical instrument. You practise for a while and sometimes you feel you're not getting anywhere. Then you do a particular exercise, movement or stroke one day and you find that your mind and body have learned it without your noticing. So whatever you do, don't let the dissatisfaction factor throw you off because you can't do everything as you want or haven't achieved the results you had dreamed of overnight. There are problems to be overcome in everything, and there are sticking points in most people's programmes: a level at which you've arrived and from where you find it hard to move. More often than not it's just your body taking a break and acclimatising itself to its new level on all systems, before it goes on to its next stage in conditioning.

Fitness levels come in stages and you just have to accept this. Don't let yourself be fooled into thinking that you must go out and double or treble your effort because you can't run a marathon or do a hundred push-ups. The criterion of your progress is how you feel, whether the exercise and diet are affecting your life beneficially on the whole and whether you honestly think you're getting more from your life than before you started.

As regards exercise gear, anything warm and loose will do. Tracksuits are ideal but if you don't have one, wear old trousers, shorts, slacks, leotard and a top – anything you like so long as you're comfortable. You can even stay in your street clothes if you wish. This will be fine for beginners because you're probably not even going to work up a sweat. So don't worry about being sweaty.

YOUR FIRST EXERCISE

This is an exercise to get your whole body moving: muscles, joints, blood, heart, lungs, everything. As a matter of fact, if you were to do this exercise alone every day of your life, for a couple of minutes, you could improve your circulation, strengthen your heart and increase the efficiency of your metabolism.

Here's what you do

1 Stand erect, feet apart.
2 Placing hands on hips, raise one knee about waist-high, rising on the ball of the other foot.
3 Now, placing the first foot back on the ground, raise the other knee, keeping on the ball of the first foot.

Do this at a slow rhythm first without ever stopping the movement. Gradually increase the pace to march-time, but never let it break into a run, where both feet are off the ground. One foot must always be on the ground.

Depending on your fitness, start at a minute, stop for thirty seconds, and do another minute. Stop for thirty seconds and do a final minute. That's three minutes effective exercise you'll have just completed.

Don't do more than this until you've been at it for about a week. Then do two two-minute sets to make a total of four minutes, with thirty-second intervals.

Keep it controlled. Don't allow the feet to run! It's not as easy as it sounds and the exercise, if done the way I've told you, will do wonders for your heart and make a start on your waistline problem if you've got one.

In the thirty-second intervals, stand straight, with your arms wrapped round yourself as in the illustration on the following   page.

4 Now, breathing in, open your arms in a wide sweeping movement, stretching your chest gently and consciously letting your shoulders move back so your shoulder blades will be coming closer together.
5 Now, breathing out, wrap your arms round yourself again in a loose sweeping movement, hunching your shoulders and squeezing your chest, leaning slightly forward.

Repeat at will. Keep the breathing in time with the movement. Keep it relaxed. Make it a loose, easy sweep, both opening the chest and closing it.

The exercise will mobilise the upper body, especially the chest or bust, and will loosen out the muscles of the shoulder and the upper back.

CONVENIENT EXERCISES FOR NATURAL RESULTS

There are some exercises which serve everyone very well. They are applicable to everyone's needs, young or old, fit or unfit, male or female. They can also be done at varying degrees of intensity and because of their versatility in this respect they are ideal for our needs here, as they can be altered in manner and degree to suit your progress.

The first will be a development of the breathing exercise outlined in the previous chapter. This has been used to strengthen and tone the stomach muscles and to aid the elimination of waste matter from the system.

1 Stand straight and at ease for a deep intake of breath.
2 Exhale completely.
3 Now bend the upper body slightly forward and place the hands on the inner thighs as illustrated on the following page. Hold the lungs empty.
4 Suck the stomach muscles up under the rib-cage as shown. Do not let air into your lungs.
5 Immediately let the stomach flop back out.

Perform this sucking and flopping action four times, then stop and breathe normally for a while.

Repeat the process, making sure your lungs are

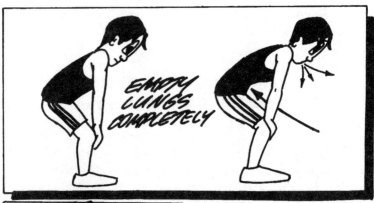

EMPTY
LUNGS
COMPLETELY

LIFT
UP
STOMACH

ABDOMINAL
LIFTS

RELAX
STOMACH
MUSCLE

completely empty before you start and that no air enters your lungs while you are doing the contractions. This exercise is invaluable to the tone of your stomach muscles, while giving your internal organs a good squeeze. It stimulates the blood-flow to this central part of the body and creates activity where normally there is little. As the alimentary canal is also squeezed and activated in a fairly vigorous manner this exercise has been known not only to reduce the waistline but also to be a wonderful aid to internal fitness and regular bowel elimination. Many people benefit greatly from this exercise, which has a great effect on their sense of wellbeing. A well-exercised abdominal area tones up the entire system. Men and women of all ages have done well with this exercise.

Overcome the temptation to do too much too soon. Keep it minimal but regular. Remember you're training for benefits, not just the sake of training. Regularity is the important thing about training in any aspect of exercise. When you are doing this exercise, bear in mind the benefits to your waistline and to your internal condition. This will motivate you to practise thoughtfully and vigorously.

What follows is a movement which capitalises on your breathing technique and developing sense of rhythm to help stimulate the circulation, accelerate elimination and invigorate and tone the heart muscle as well as the other organs in the body. Do take it easy. Too frequently a fast charge at the exercise gives an unnecessary soreness. In some cases this can mean doing little or nothing for a week or so afterwards, so you end up back where you started. Start lightly and increase your intensity and activity as your agility allows. It is a fact that a vigorous exercise session may be more beneficial in itself than a mild one. But it is a more relevant fact that milder sessions regularly done are infinitely more valuable than the hit-and-miss approach.

Your muscles and system will more easily take to the habit when they are trained rather than strained.

A regular and light exercise session will have an effect on your system that an inlet and outlet will have on a stagnant pond. It will keep it free, clear and clean. When the same water lies in a pond unchanged, gathering the droppings of birds, trees and anything else that falls or crawls into it, it becomes stagnant and will not support life. However, if you put an inlet and outlet on the pond, the residue is washed away and the clean water brings life and vitality back to the pond.

So it is with your bloodstream. If it is given regular and adequate even if light dose of fresh oxygen it will support you and help you live better. It will nourish your bones, muscle, nerves and brain more efficiently. It will keep dirt from accumulating in your system and you will see the improvement in the condition of your skin and hair.

SQUAT

This exercise has all the ingredients that go to make a first-class overall toner and strengthener. It has been used by both athletes and beauty queens, and is a wonderful exercise for a sound development of the heart and the lungs. It is called the squat. But you have to do it right so that the desired effect is produced.

1 Stand erect with both your heels on a slight rise.
2 Keeping your back flat and your shoulders back and making sure that your heels stay in contact with the supports you have placed under them, lower your body till your thighs are roughly parallel to the floor.
3 Keeping the heels on the supports, press against the

supports till your legs are straight again and you have returned to the starting position.

4 Breathe in as you descend and breathe out as you straighten back up again.

Always try to coordinate the breathing with the movement so that you develop a rhythm and concentration in your programme. If you find it difficult to descend to the parallel at first, don't become disheartened; go as far as you comfortably can so as not to strain anything. Your muscles will quickly get into the habit of the movement and in a short time you will be able to do the exercise as prescribed. Don't rush it. You may also find it difficult to keep your heels on the supports at first. A bit of practice will overcome the problem.

Once you get the hang of the basic movement you can do six to eight repetitions in a steady easy style, running one movement into the next so that there is no discernible pause between them. This is a good way of keeping the tension on the muscles and helping to speed up the results.

After some practice the repetitions can be increased until you have a steady rhythmic performance of twenty. You will notice not only a feeling of exertion in the thighs but also, when the exercise is done in a lively manner, an effect on the heart as it pumps the blood through. This activity brings the rate of your heartbeat up, so that the heart is being exercised too. As you continue your other movements after the squat you will be able to feel the increase in the number of heartbeats per minute by putting your hand on your breast. Provided you don't get the heart beating too quickly too soon, this will benefit you enormously. Your heart as a result of light but regular training will respond like any other muscle and get fitter and stronger. The great advantage here is that it will then do more work with a lot less effort. This is why people who have had heart attacks and associated troubles are regularly given a light exercise programme instead of being told to lie in bed.

When it rests and does nothing, the heart, just like any other little-used muscle, loses its tone and activity. It merely has to work sufficiently to circulate the blood in a body heedless of nutrition and oxygen. So when a sudden and unexpected demand is made upon it, it may not have the strength or conditioning to cope – with disastrous results.

On the other hand, a regularly exercised heart provides the body with a constant supply of necessary oxygen and food nourishment, with wonderful results. That may sound excessive but it's true. Personal energy is of course a personal characteristic. But if you have an idea, a plan, an ambition, a dream, all the wishful thinking in the world won't get it for you without the basic steps being taken. That frequently needs more than just a bit of organising and setting up. It needs physical and mental application, steadfastness, perseverance, not just at the outset or at the finish, but in the middle too. When the going is tough, that is when the energy, the application and the action is needed. As nineteenth-century author Samuel Smiles wrote:

> The most important results in daily life are to be obtained, not through the exercise of extraordinary powers such as genius and intellect, but through the the energetic use of simple means and ordinary qualities, with which nearly all human individuals have been more or less endowed.

Samuel Smiles's book *Self Help* was first published in 1859.

Your exercises may have a greater effect on your life than just making you a bit fitter. They can be part of a programme is a whole new way of life. You can make them an integral part of a plan for what you intend to be and do in your life. Only *you* can do it, no one can stop you. Your exercises can be the physical expression of the most exciting decision of your life -to change your lot. The decision is yours.

OVERHEAD STRETCH

Our next movement is to gently stretch the body, letting the muscles, joints, spine, all stretch gently out, so that the weight of gravity is taken off them and they can settle and rest into their proper positions.

This exercise is wonderful for people who have let their posture get out of alignment. It will gently mobilise joints and muscles. It will also realign the breathing apparatus. Improved circulation and vitality will result, along with a sense of physical comfort.

1 First, stand in the proper posture.
2 With hands in front of your waist, back to back, e-a-s-e them up over your head. Keep standing with your feet flat on the floor.
3 S-t-r-e-t-c-h comfortably, your fingers reaching to the ceiling, till you can go no further. Hold this position briefly, imagining you are being pulled up to the ceiling by your wrists.
4 Let your arms down gently, moving as gracefully as you can, to the starting position.

Repeat this five times.

When you're more advanced and confident, you can extend the technique to raise and stretch from the toes.

This does take practice. It also requires concentration to keep the sequence fluid and smooth. It is, however, very relaxing and it acts as a great decongestant of all the organs and lungs. Its effect on the circulation is deep. It is a fine mental refresher, specially useful for students or workers at a desk. A two-minute break to do this exercise will help refocus your concentration.

Remember, e-a-s-e into and out of the movement. Take your time. Get the feel of it for the first few days. Practice will improve concentration and your sense of balance. Don't rush it. Let it take its own time.

FORWARD HANG

After the overhead stretch, it's a good idea to effect a gentle resettlement of the back and front muscles of the upper body. This will take advantage of the stretched spine and help develop a suppleness in the back, the hips and the backs of the legs.

1 Stand straight and at ease as described earlier.
2 Keeping your legs barely bent at the knee, allow your upper body to come forward, your arms hanging loose in front of you. (Do not force this. Just hang forward so you place no strain on anything. Stay loose. The operative word here is hang. That is what your upper body is doing: hanging. Let your hands hang towards your feet, loosely.)
3 Return to the standing position, slowly, with e-a-s-e.
4 Bring your shoulders back as you've learned before, letting the shoulder blades come towards each other. Breath freely.
5 Move gently forward again, relaxing and loosening, so

STANDING STRAIGHT

SLIGHT BEND IN KNEE

STRAIGHTEN SLOWLY

your upper body hangs comfortably in front of your pelvic area. Then return it smoothly back again to the upright position.

6 Repeat this five times, never rushing, never speeding up, nor slowing down, but keeping a loose and easy gentle movement all the time.

Time and practice will pay dividends. You will be mobilising the body, activating the muscular system and having a great effect on the circulation. Your organs will also get a good toning. Your energy will be helped enormously.

HIP HONER

The next exercise is one which must be of great interest to anyone wishing to keep the hips in good shape. All too frequently the muscles of the buttocks become soft and flabby, with dire effects on appearance, especially for those in sedentary jobs. This is because fat tends to gather around unused muscle: the muscle goes soft and fat builds up. Combined with the pressure and natural restriction to the blood-flow caused by sitting down, this causes the area to be virtually starved of life-giving oxygen. Positive and regular action must be taken to alleviate this. If you find yourself sitting all day, take hourly leg-stretches and walks around your desk or office. It won't interfere with your work. If anything it will improve your performance as it will help prevent stagnation and sluggishness.

1 Move to the hands and knees position.
2 Gently extend one leg behind you, keeping the leg comfortably straight and just higher than your buttocks.
3 Hold the leg like this for a few moments and then return it to the floor.

LEG STRAIGHT PROGRESSIVELY

SLOWLY LOWERED RETURNING TO ORIGINAL POSITION

4 Repeat four to five times with each leg, making sure that the leg is held just higher than the buttocks.

This will ensure a wonderful contraction on the muscle of the buttocks. Done regularly it will stimulate the blood-flow, tighten the tissue and produce firm well-shaped buttocks. If you've difficulty raising your leg or straightening it at first, don't force it. Just do what you can in comfort. You may find too that one leg lifts more easily than the other. This is often the case. It can be the result of many factors: personal balance, strength, old injuries, posture. Don't worry about this; just raise each leg within its own comfort range. Regular practice will bring rewards.

Do two to three lifts when you're starting. As you progress, you will find your own optimum number. Some people leave it at five or ten repetitions. Others will do fifteen or twenty. It's important to discover what's comfortable and effective for you. As you get familiar with the movement, you'll also find that your sense of balance improves. This will have a clear effect on your performance.

WAIST SHAVER

Just over the side of the hip is a relatively small but very important muscle. Around this can gather a roll of fat which makes itself apparent on even a thin person. It is important to develop the condition of these muscles. As well as keeping the waist trim by precise exercise, they provide coordination between the upper and lower parts of the body, when in tone giving an easy agility to walking and running. This is an invaluable asset to anyone who spends a lot of time standing or walking. This exercise will help to reduce fatigue and the low spirits it causes.

1   Keeping the elbows back and the palms on the hips, lean the body over as far as it will comfortably go to the right side.
2   Return to an erect position and repeat six to ten times in a slow and rhythmic fashion. Let your breath come and go as it pleases but breathe through the nose.
3   Do the same for the left side, all the time taking care to keep the elbows back and the spine straight.

If you do the exercise in front of a mirror and observe yourself, you will be able to pay attention to the details of execution. Develop it to twenty-five to thirty times per session for each side. But take your time and don't rush either the daily progress or the rhythm of the movement. After a while you can move smoothly from left to right, keeping a steady easy pace, with no perceptible pause at either right or left sides, moving steadily from one repetition into the next, staying loose and relaxed, calm and smooth.

Have the feet about shoulder-width apart and the legs fairly straight. Don't let the knees dip with each movement. Keep the legs steady and the movement smooth, with no jerking.

As well as shaping and trimming the waist, this exercise helps suppleness in the back and flexes the hips and legs.

GOOD MORNING

This is a great exercise to aid circulation, improve suppleness and strengthen the muscles of the upper hip and back. It will also stretch the backs of the legs and add tone to the hamstrings (back of thighs) and calves – parts very often neglected.

1 Lean back as far as you comfortably can, doing this slowly and breathing in through your nose as you do so. Fill your lungs completely.
2 Lower your trunk to the indicated forward position, as you exhale through the mouth, ridding your lungs of any air.

This movement must be done in a slow concentrated manner, coordinating the breathing with the activity - breathing in as you slowly lean back, breathing out as you bend forward. Keep your legs apart and slightly bent at all times.

SELF-REFRESHER

This final exercise is about as close as you will come to the efforts of the mystic experts. Its purpose is to let the blood and body take advantage of the fact of gravity to help refresh the mind and revitalise the system.

When this exercise is put into daily practice, with the right attitude, tension, unnecessary fears and anxiety tend to retreat. A more positive and constructive thought-process begins to assert itself in daily living.

1 Lie flat on the floor on your back, with your hands under your buttocks.
2 Bring your knees right up to your chest.
3 Place your hands underneath the small of your back or your hips, supporting your weight.
4 Slowly straighten both legs up into the air, pointing your toes to the ceiling, still supporting your hips with your forearms.
5 Breathe slowly and rhythmically through your nose,

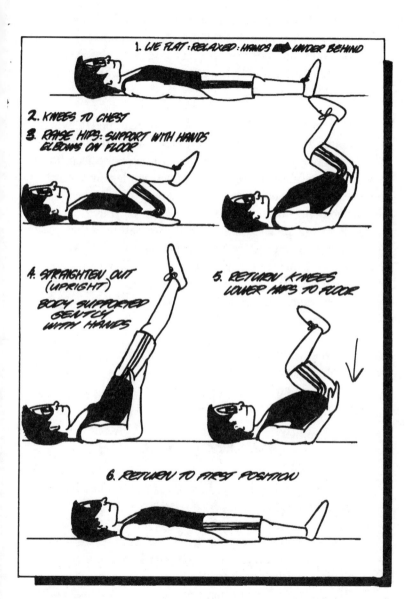

concentrating on the total stillness of both feet pointed as near as possible directly towards the ceiling.

6 Maintain the position for as long as comfortably possible, then slowly lower your legs and hips to the flat lying position.

With practice you will find that you will be able to maintain this position indefinitely and that your concentration will remain unbroken. You will also learn to hold yourself more erect and your back and legs will keep the vertical more easily so that after a time the only parts of your body in contact with the ground will be your elbows, shoulders and the back of your head. This ensures a flow of blood to the brain and the other upper regions of the body, which, no matter how well your heart is pumping, do not get enough blood if you are on your feet all day. It also frees the lower limbs of accumulated blood. This helps to stop clotting and can be useful in preventing varicose veins.

The refreshing qualities alone of this movement have to be experienced to be appreciated. Hundreds of members in our club in Dublin practise this at home as a tension reliever. It is used by a lot of people to overcome the longing for sugary foods when they first go on a reducing diet.

TUMMY TONER

Here is the exercise that has helped to flatten thousands of bulging tummies.

1 Lie flat on the floor, arms flat along the body, palms on thighs. Gently raise your head and reach along your body, as if trying to touch your knees.

2 Slowly, gently, return to start position.

3 Breathe freely. Your stomach muscles will tense and

LIE FLAT DOWN ON FLOOR

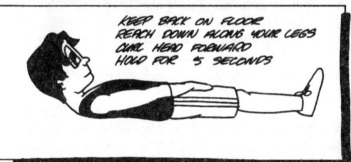

HANDS FLAT - (PALMS ON THIGHS)

KEEP BACK ON FLOOR
REACH DOWN ALONG YOUR LEGS
CURL HEAD FORWARD
HOLD FOR 5 SECONDS

RETURN TO FIRST POSITION

tighten. This will firm them and tone up the organs in your system. Hold for a count of five. Repeat this three times. If you feel any discomfort, stop after the first. Over the weeks, increase the number of repetitions to five, holding each tension for a count of five.

CHEST TONER/BUST CONDITIONER

There are two stages in this movement;

Stage 1
1   The first is the hands-and-knees movement, with the palms of the hands slightly in front of you.
2   Now slowly lower your chest to the floor. You will come slightly forward, letting your chest just tip the floor, keeping your head up.
3   Return to full hands-and-knees position.

Do this slowly and smoothly. Don't let it get fast and jerky. Keep a steady fluid movement, letting each repetition flow into the next. When you've got this up to from twenty to twenty-five repetitions, in total control, you can move on to stage two.

Stage 2
1   Straighten out on hands and toes, hands about shoulder-width apart.
2   Slowly, lower yourself, touching the floor with your chest.
3   Without pausing, press yourself back to the start position. Do this two to three times. Do it well. Do not go for a high number of repetitions. Just concentrate on doing the perfect movement, slowly, smoothly, fluently.

BACK FLAT: HANDS SLIGHTLY IN FRONT

GENTLY LOWER YOUR CHEST TO THE FLOOR

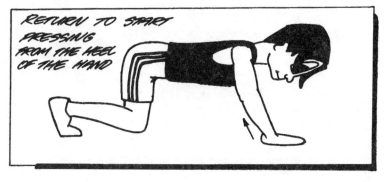

RETURN TO START PRESSING FROM THE HEEL OF THE HAND

BRING CHEST TO FLOOR

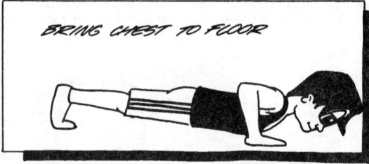

RETURN TO FIRST POSITION

Add one repetition per week. If you feel that at five to ten repetitions you've enough, that's fine Don't try to increase the number you're doing, but do them regularly.

After some months you may feel like increasing the number to fifteen, twenty or even more. If so, fine, but again, concentrate on how you're doing them, not on how many you're doing.

Even when you're fit and trim, there will be times when you'll do only a few because you're tired, concerned or preoccupied with some aspect in your life. Don't lose heart and think you're failing in your fitness programme. Everyone has off-days. See them as that and leave it there. At other times you'll feel as if you could go on forever. Concentrate on regularity. This is the key factor. Like life, every course has its ups and downs, and the one who gets there is the one who stays on it.

PURIFYING BREATH

To finish, I suggest a simple breathing exercise to flush the system with oxygen. This need only take a couple of minutes at the most.

1 Stand straight and relaxed.
2 Breathe in deeply and slowly as you've learned, through the nose.
3 Without holding your breath, blow all the air out gently, tensing your stomach muscles.
4 As soon as your lungs are empty, let the air drift in again through your nose, smoothly moving from inhalation to exhalation.

Ten to twenty breaths like this will open the lungs and flush your system with oxygen, giving the circulation a real boost. It will also help prevent any tendency to soreness. The oxygen in your bloodstream, from this and your other breathing exercises, will combust the toxins, wastes and lactic acid which might otherwise accumulate and cause the stiffness people often experience after exercising.

Always finish with these breathing exercises.

INTENSITY

It is recommended that the foregoing exercises be done five days a week. If you are reasonably fit and can do a high number of repetitions of each one, you may prefer to do them at a time when it's convenient to have a shower after them. Make no mistake: this workout, although it may be tackled in a gentle way by a man or woman who has rarely, if ever, exercised, may also be vigorously undertaken by a fit person and used to work up a sweat. You can increase the vigour and intensity of application as you progress in fitness.

A point worth bearing in mind is that you may find different levels of performance at different sessions or a preference for one exercise today and another tomorrow. Many factors may influence this.

'A healthy mind in a healthy body' is not some meaningless cliché. Research over the years has shown that people are more alert, resourceful, persistent and creative when they become more active. Physically fit men are 53 per cent less at risk of premature death and physically fit women are 98 per cent less at risk of premature death than sedentary men and women. (Source: Blair and Kohl, *Journal of the American Medical Association,* November 1989.)

As to problems, they have to be faced. Acknowledging them as problems often helps solve them but many people live in a state of apprehension, looking for something to to worry about. Such an attitude will permeate every aspect of your life and shade every syllable you utter, taking the force and confidence from your exercise activity and rendering it next to useless.

In order to overcome this, apply yourself mentally to your exercises with maximum concentration. This is one way of ridding your mind of unnecessary fears and replacing them with strong and positive attitudes. Your exercise session will in this way not only be a physically strengthening and refreshing practice but a mental revitalisation as well.

SLEEP AND EXERCISE

You may find occasionally that in spite of the physical ability to exercise and even the desire to do it it's very difficult actually to apply yourself. A frequent reason for this is lack of sleep. Our need for sleep varies. Under pressure, when we're working harder than usual or after a crisis, we usually require more sleep than when everything's going along as we intended. When we're under pressure, our creative energies are directed more forcefully to the survival aspects of life. Unimportant things are seen for what they are and the eagerness with which we approach our daily lives takes an immoderate toll on our reserves. In order to maintain a normal and balanced outlook we need more sleep than usual, and it should be uninterrupted sleep. For the same reasons we need solid sleep when working harder than normal.

During a crisis, we tend to dwell upon the various angles

of the problem when we should be getting a good night's sleep. Problem times and critical times tend to drain your energy. A lot of solutions come in sleep, when the difficulties have been handed over to the subconscious for solving. The solution is usually dredged up some time in the day following a good night's sleep.

This is not to say that at the first sign of trouble in your life you have to drop everything and dive between the sheets, pretending the problem doesn't exist, and that you will miraculously awaken with the problem solved – though this belief seems to have its followers. Nor is it to say that the only thing in the world to knock you off form for exercising is lack of sleep.

Lack of sleep, particularly in our society, where late TV, late shows, late callers and late parties play such a prominent part in many lives, is worth considering as a possible factor when you're feeling a bit off and generraly find everything you have to do is a chore.

Psychologists are very clear about this. The first couple of hours of sleep are those in which any dreaming is done and this is an important factor in mental readjustment during the night. This part of the sleep cycle is characterised by flickering of the eyes – Rapid Eye Movement (REM) – and after this comes the deep physically refreshing slumber which leaves us fresh and ready for the next day.

People's requirements vary enormously but one thing is certain: too many people do not get enough sleep. If you think that there might be the slightest chance that you are being so affected, have a few early nights as soon as possible. Not just one – a few. Reschedule your appointments, dates or journeys and make sure you get more sleep than you normally get at present. Don't just try it for a night, or a week or even two to three weeks. Do it for at least six weeks, and if the benefit is apparent in your life –

if you have more energy, improved concentration, sounder nerves and a greater sense of wellbeing, stick to the new schedule.

When you are engaged in an exercise programme there is one element which could arguably take priority over all others as the key to success. This is regularity in performance. A lot of people will take this for granted but there are others who see exercises as something to be done in a few minutes at odd times during the course of the month. A light session, possible even for the very unfit, should be done at least once daily.

It is important to carry out the session at a time that suits you. When an experienced runner, for instance, says that the best time to train is at 6 am, he's talking about his own personal preference. He will be able to give you very valid reasons and sound so thoroughly convincing that he will persuade you that to train at any other time is useless. You could get up at 6 am for a few mornings and do a workout or a run or a breathing programme and a walk, but though you might feel better for your activity, you could also experience fatigue or depression or loss of appetite or irritability. The experienced runner may have omitted to tell you that he's in bed by 10.30 or 11 five nights a week or that he has cultivated the habit of napping for a half-hour every second afternoon. Generally speaking, any time is the right time to exercise – as long as it suits you. Don't be afraid to experiment to see how you feel and how different times suit your lifestyle.

This affair of timing is important. If you find that a particular time of day suits you for some reason you can't define, keep to that time. You will enjoy your training more, put more into it and benefit accordingly. Mental attitude also has to do with this aspect of training. One person may feel that he is starting the day right with a symbolic and actual cleansing, inside and out, with his exercise session and shower. Another may feel the need of a symbolic catharsis after a day's work and before s/he goes home to the family. Yet another may feel the need for both – a wind-up and a relaxing of the spring of tension.

EXERCISE, PERSPIRATION AND SORENESS

A great number of people think you have to sweat profusely every time you train in order to benefit from your workout. They may also think that if you're not aching all over the next day, afraid to laugh or cough for the consequent agony, that you haven't trained sufficiently.

Get this right, now. Sweat and pain are not necessary to developing fundamental fitness. Remember what we said about the breathing exercises earlier: they are the basis of your whole programme.

Sweating is your body's way of keeping you reasonably cool so that you can function efficiently. It usually comes as a result of (relatively) intense activity. It also eliminates waste through the skin. So if you do get active enough to work up a sweat during your exercise, well and good; it certainly won't harm you – but don't make the mistake of having a lather of perspiration your objective. It is not necessarily the measurement of merit in a training session. Conditions and personal aspects have a bearing on the matter. On a hot day an overweight person will perspire heavily from the very start of the workout. A fit and trim person can run for a considerable distance in winter and hardly show a trace of sweat. A person who trains for a short time but makes himself pant, on a regular basis, will benefit far more than another, who trains every now and again and sweats profusely.

Soreness is usually caused by a build-up of waste from the muscles. If you haven't trained or played a game for some time and then go out one day and give yourself a tough physical workout, you may expect a degree of soreness. The interesting thing about it is that it won't be the day after that you are really sore but the one following that. The situation comes about something like this.

You're sitting in your office all week. On Friday evening you're invited to make up a position on the club team for Sunday because the regular is sick. You accept. You go and you play. During the course of your game a lot of accumulated wastes and toxins are shuttled out of their recesses, shaken up and dislodged. But they are not eliminated from your system. Lactic acid is produced from your muscles during your play and if it is not eliminated either it lodges at what are termed the origins and insertions of the muscles – that is to say, the tendons which join the muscles to the various bones.

These disturbed wastes and acids settle during the following day's relative inactivity and inhibit muscular movement. The result on the third day can be great soreness in moving. In extreme cases people have been virtually paralysed. Practically everyone has experienced discomfort and pain in varying degrees as the result of the type of situation outlined above.

When this occurs, there is little joy in togging out to go for another training session. Even those hardies who feel that they have to be even a bit sore to give merit to a workout will admit that they function more efficiently when they are pain-free. Everyone does. A more enlightened approach than heretofore prevails in fitness instruction today and as a direct result a lot more people are enjoying training and contributing to their communal sports activities as well as to their own fitness and happiness.

If training is started lightly and kept to within the individual's rate of performance, with an eye to regular increase in effort – however small – the results will be positive and, just as important, enjoyably achieved. Never doubt it.

EXERCISE, CONFIDENCE AND SEX

Without going into intimate details, and without trying for a moment to advise on the various factors that can cause psycho-sexual problems, let's briefly mention the value of fitness and hygiene where sex is concerned. If you are looking and feeling your best, whatever your best may be, you will have confidence, which allows you to think constructively and frees your limbs, muscles and nervous system from the dysfunction that a negative and fearful attitude can engender. Confidence is one of those invaluable intangibles than no man or woman can live effectively without.

From the purely physical point of view, personal hygiene and fitness can greatly improve a mediocre sex life. A body that is fatigued, out of sorts, run down and lethargic cannot enjoy itself as much as if it were fit and strong. A body that's flabby, out of shape and uncared for may not be attracting the kind of attention its owner would like it to be attracting.

If you are at ease with your body and confident that you've given it your best attention and got the best from it, it cannot but help you to be confident in all areas of life, and sex is no exception.

EXERCISE AND SMOKING

If you read the papers regularly you'll be aware of the significance attached to smoking in the occurrence of cancer. It's pretty well agreed the world over by leading authorities that smoking is a great danger to health. It also has a profound effect on the heart, as any cardiac surgeon will tell you.

Apart from these aspects, there is one other point about smoking which will interest you. This is something that is not generally thought about and is very important where your fitness is concerned. When you draw on a cigarette, the gas which comes up along to the mouth from the white ash is carbon monoxide. This gas is inhaled into the lungs and then passed into the blood which is filtering through the air sacs. This means that a poisonous gas is being sent into the lungs, displacing the essential oxygen. Yes, carbon monoxide is poisonous. That's what comes out in a car's exhaust fumes. That's what a considerable number of suicides use when they decide they've had enough of this old world and want to get out of it.

Cigarette smokers do the same. They inhale the poison and prevent the oxygen from getting into the bloodstream. They may be assured too that the poison will be efficiently passed around the system, thereby adding to the waste that is already there, because of the fact that the heart, which pumps the blood, is stimulated by the nicotine from the cigarette.

Another interesting point is the fact that the blood cells used to carry the gas are rendered useless for at least twelve hours. So you are effectively reducing the amount of blood in your body by smoking. It's no wonder that smokers experience doziness, cramps, agonising breathlessness and weakness when they attempt to exercise.

EXERCISE AND YOUR LIFE

If you are sound in wind and limb, if you have normal
mental and emotional activity, you owe it to yourself,
your family, your boss, your employees, your country and
your community to protect that precious health and grab
whatever means are available to keep the machine
running smoothly. Do an analysis of your lifestyle. If you
have habits that jeopardise your own happiness or that of
others, it is worth considering change – if not a complete
change, then maybe a modification. Whatever decision
you may make about your lifestyle you will be taking a
very noticeable and direct step forward if you give yourself a regular dose of exercise. If nothing else, exercise,
sensibly and moderately undertaken, will have a positive
and definite effect on your system if you are overweight
or suffer the effects of too much tobacco and alcohol.

5

RELAXATION

Relaxation is fundamental to good health. It is a relatively simple thing to establish an effective relaxation system in our lives. If we don't take this step, stress, tension, worry and fear can fill our days, creeping in unnoticed till they pervade destructively every part of our lives.

In recent years, stress has been recognised for the insidious evil that it is. Many of us have suffered from it, unaware of what it was till someone gave it a name. Then we looked and said, 'Yes, that's me. I'm the tired one. I'm the fatigued one. I'm the one who feels run down and out of sorts. Can't sleep at night, can't work at day. I don't feel ill but can't say I'm well. There are things I want to do. Places I want to go. Levels I want to reach. And I know I've got the capability. I know I can do it. I know the potential is within me. I've done things before. I can do them again.'

'One day. Some day. Not to day. Maybe tomorrow? Or the day after? Some day! Soon.' Sound familiar?

Fear, worry, stress are barriers to action. They wound people, tear them apart and leave them floundering, aimless. Worry and anxiety don't just affect our minds; we worry too in our hearts, our brains, our guts. Fear and worry, one American surgeon said, can be noted in the very cells, tissues and organs of the body.

And we really know this. We know the tight feeling in the gut when anxiety sinks in. We know the knots of tension that can build and tighten the shoulders till they grip like a vice round the neck and sear in blinding pain through the head.

It wasn't for nothing that expressions such as 'It's a pain in the neck' – or 'This is one real headache' came about. The physical discomfort that stress brings is well catalogued and experienced by everyone from the school student doing difficult homework to the top financier running a multi-million-pound business. The homemaker, the accountant, the road worker, the farmer, people in all walks of life experience stress. Indeed the walk of life in which you find yourself is largely irrelevant. Once anxiety sets in, its toll is as debilitating for one person as it is for the next.

There was a time when stress was thought of as only affecting what we term as high achievers, people who push themselves to extreme limits to reach goals. But now we know better. We know any life can be subjected to stress, or to be more precise, distress. Just think of the typical day of the working person. He or she wakes up, we'll say, to the relentless call of the alarm at a quarter to seven. It takes two, maybe three minutes to come awake and acknowledge the day. Another few minutes are spent getting together clothes to wear. If the worker is a man, he goes to the bathroom for shower, shampoo and shave. As he does his teeth there's a dimly flashing alarm in the back of his mind reminding him of the likely traffic conditions on the way to work. As he dresses he flicks on the radio to get the news, weather, traffic conditions. Down the stairs into the kitchen, kettle on, still buttoning shirt sleeves, tie draped over shoulder to be fitted and knotted. He stops everything to listen to a dramatic news item; then carries on, still half aware of weather, traffic reports and time checks. All of a sudden it's half-seven instead of twenty past. He throws on a jacket, slurps a mouthful of tea and charges out the door. Into the car, switches it on. Won't start. It's cold. Needs more choke. Pulls out the choke. Tries again. Nearly starts. Maybe too much choke. Shoves it back in a bit. Foot lightly on the accelerator, try now. Fine. She starts. Turn on the radio. Twenty-five to eight. The fellow says so. That's far too late. Leave the house at half-seven and you're in the city and parked by eight-thirty. You've time to get yourself set for the day. Leave the house at twenty-five to eight and you won't get to town till ten to nine, look for a parking space and the phones are ringing and there are people looking for you as you burst through the door already behind schedule. Your stress levels are making your heart race, making your breathing shallow and poisoning your mind with a strong foreboding of what the rest of the day may bring. And that's only the start.

If we're to prevent this wrecking our entire day, we have to use whatever methods of dispersion of this stress that are available to us. There are two significant points to bear in mind here. The first is that in the instance just mentioned, we are capable of preventing the stress by getting up a bit earlier, having everything done in time, thus removing the source of the stress.

But there will be other instances where the source will be outside our control, in which case we can do nothing about that. What we can do is control our reaction to it.

There is a prayer used in the Alcoholics Anonymous movement which could be well applied to any of our lives:

God grant me the serenity to accept what I cannot change, the courage to change the things I can, and the wisdom to know the difference.

There will always be thorns in our sides from outside sources. We may not be able to do too much about them but we will always be able to do something about our attitude to, perception of, and reaction to these difficulties.

The constant tensions, the negatives in life, the condition of hopelessness to which we can so easily succumb, can, if we let them, bind us up mentally and emotionally and render us virtually helpless in the face of any adversity. As Shakespeare wrote hundreds of years ago: 'Our doubts are traitors and make us lose the good we oft might win, by fearing to attempt.'

Or we can change all that.

There are a couple of things we have to acknowledge. The first is that a certain amount of stress is necessary. This is what gives us the impetus to get up in the morning, go to work, earn a living. Also, in times of crisis, it gives us the urgency to bring out the stamina, courage, persistence to deal with adversity and overcome it. But there is the different kind that does us no good at all. This might more correctly be called distress.

A lot of the damaging stress comes from the smaller difficulties in life. Not that they're as harmful in themselves as the greater ones, but that they tend to get overlooked and simmer underneath the surface of our lives. They accumulate. After a while we adapt to the state of stress. We become tense, irritable, feel run-down but because we've become accustomed to it, we accept it as a normal condition. And that is the vital word: 'condition'. We let ourselves become conditioned to stress. We have unconsciously taught ourselves stress.

We have been unconsciously willing students. We have learned how to be tense, tired during the day, too tired to sleep at night, to have poor digestion, to be constipated, to eat and drink too much as a way of to eat and drink too much as a way of comfort, to be narky, fretful, constantly anxious for some unknown reason, shuffling through life in a state of tired confusion, not sick, but never really well. After a while we accept this as our normal state.

We even regard people who are naturally relaxed and at ease (or seem to be) as unusual, even suspect. When people don't overreact to a shock, mental or physical, we label them as 'cold fish', or 'cool ones' and not in a complimentary tone.

But change is coming. Not only are the psychologists and spiritual counsellors now talking of the reality of stress, so are the medics. And even the press interprets the phenomenon as serious fact, and not a notion to wonder about and forget.

The physical consequences of stress have been well documented. Tranquillisers don't solve the problem. Neither do drugs. There has been a move over the past few years towards the teaching and use of natural relaxation techniques. These not only help the stress victim to get rid of symptoms of disease but commonly get down to the source of the problem as well. There are many variations of technique. I've no intention here of arguing which is most effective. They all come from a common basis anyway. So if you learn the basis then you can modify it any way you want to suit yourself. If it works for you use it. That is the only criterion by which you measure whether it's right or wrong. The only thing you do have to commit to is the same as in the other chapters: regularity.

Like your breathing exercises, your toning movements, your posture points, you have to put these techniques into practice.

You will now teach yourself the opposite of what you have allowed yourself to become; to be relaxed, at ease, unhurried and calm. It doesn't mean you won't have problems in life. You will. But your reaction will be calm

and you will cope. Even knowing that you can cope, that the problem is surmountable, is often enough to help you alter the circumstances or overcome them altogether.
So with this aim in mind, that of taking control of our lives, and developing our own aims, let's get started.

GROUND RULES FOR SUCCESS

- First: resolve on regularity in what you practise. Determine to do it, quietly, effectively.
- Second: keep your practice private, to yourself. Do it at a time and in a place where you will have no fear of criticism, demands on your attention or any other type of interruption.
- Third: make sure that the room in which you do it is quiet. Get used to listening to your own silence. Become familiar with the stillness. Don't be afraid of it. Don't be afraid of your own thoughts. Decide what you want to put into your mind. Then let silence and persistence prevail in which those thoughts and their direction can take hold.
- Fourth: keep warm. You must be comfortable when letting yourself go quiet. This is not usually a problem in summer, unless you're in a draught. If you're starting in winter you may need a room warmed by fire or heating or even have to to use a blanket.
- Fifth: when starting your relaxation periods, you may find yourself falling asleep. Don't worry about that. A relaxed, self-induced snooze away from the rush and bustle of daily life won't do you any harm.
  Some of the most famous and powerful people in history developed the technique of cat-napping as a remedy for fatigue, John F. Kennedy and Winston Churchill to name two.

In the classes I give, many people regard their developed ability to catch a quick sleep during the day as the most valuable achievement in their courses. It is a good way to halt your day and recharge the batteries.

After practising, you will be able to relax with your mind calm and yet be aware of everything going on around you. This may sound contradictory but it is the chief benefit, as you are then developing the ability to distance yourself from events which would normally affect your mind and emotions. So, assuming that you have taken all the foregoing on board, let's get started.

Lie on the floor, totally flat. Let your head and shoulders have easy and equal contact with the floor. Let your back and buttocks lie comfortably, with your arms resting along by your sides, palms facing up. The palms-up position may feel a bit awkward at first. But if you allow the forearm to have contact with the floor, you will find that the fingers can relax more easily, finding their own curvature and letting the entire hand experience relaxation. This is more important than is generally realised. Among the most tense parts of your body, are hands and fingers. It is necessary to have them in a position in which they will have no inhibition in relaxing. If your hands are palms-down, the movement of fingers and wrist may be inhibited by contact with the floor. Palms-up will let your hands be naturally in their own particular individual shape.

The palms-up is also a submissive position and has a far more profound psychological effect than we are prepared to acknowledge. There is a certain openness about it, which is conducive to trusting the process we are about to undertake.

If we're to go along with the idea that relaxation is really a lack of tension, then we'll use the following procedure to achieve it.

BODY FLAT

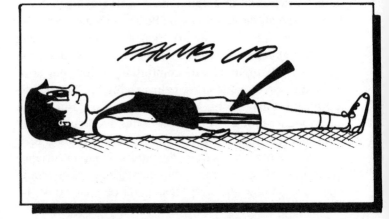

PALMS UP

RELAXED
L·O·O·S·E

You're lying on the floor, at ease, comfortable, loose.

You won't realise it but there are still some knots of tension in your body. They've been gathering there for years, and you have become so accustomed to feeling them you don't even recognise them any more.

Slowly curl your toes away from you. Slowly. Let your feet curl away so they get slightly tense. Be aware of the tension in your feet. Feel it. Hold the tightness so it's beyond the state of comfort. Your feet will be tense, taut, tight. And you will be aware of this tension.

Now slowly release the tension. Let the feet and toes straighten and let the feet flop out and relax. Feel the difference. Be aware of the relaxation, the looseness, in toes and feet. Feel the relaxed warmth and ease in your feet. Wriggle the toes. Leave the feet loose. Think of the looseness. Focus your thoughts on the ease and comfort of the toes and feet.

Now, slowly, start to curl the feet back towards you. Curl the toes. Feel the heel stretch away from you as you do this. Feel the tension in the calves of your legs. They are stretching, tightening, going tense. Hold that tension. Focus on it. Fill your mind with the feeling and the sight of your calves going taut and tense. Be aware of the intensity of this stretching. Feel it. Force it. Feel the discomfort and force the heel away from you. Push the heel and curl the toes back towards you.

Now slowly release the tension from the calves and let the feet straighten and loosen and flop as they did before; feel the tension leaving the calves and the feet and the ankles as they lie in relief from the tension you have imposed on them. Now they are loose, loose and relaxed and lying quietly and heavily on the floor. You will now be aware of the difference between the tension and the relaxation you have brought about.

Now bring your mind up to your thighs. Be aware of how you're lying. Focus the mind on your thighs. See them in your mind. They are lying quietly. Doing nothing else. At ease.

Start to tense them. Focus. Concentrate. Fill your mind with the gradually tightening thighs, getting tenser by the second. See the muscle, slowly getting very, very tense, tightening the whole upper leg into immobility. There is discomfort coming into the thigh, keeping the leg rigid so the knees and all the limbs are totally fixed by the force of your tension. You are aware of the rigidity and discomfort of this maximum force of tension as you exert it.

Now release it. Feel the tension dropping away and the comfort flooding into your legs as the muscle loosens and the knees ease and the whole of the legs relax in ease and sink in comfort and relief on to the floor.

You will now have grasped the pattern: tighten, think, loosen, think. The power of the procedure is in the thought. It is a mental exercise. The thought makes the tension and focuses on the relief. It is a neuromuscular exercise in contrasts. It has to be intellectually active to be effective. Concentration is the key. It is not the passive going through the motions that most people think it is. If you've followed so far what I've instructed you to do, you will have experienced the difference in tension and lack of it to a degree you may never have experienced before. As you practise, it will become even more noticeable and the sense of relaxation you will feel will be nothing short of delicious.

The next part to focus on is your buttocks. As with the other parts, focus your mind on the body part involved. Your buttocks. Thought is all. Gently, begin to squeeze the buttocks so they are starting to tense. Keep increasing this tension, slowly. This is vital, to develop a gradual, easy tension into the muscular area you have targeted in your mind. Concentrate, not just on the body part, but on the gradually increasing tension as you tighten the cheeks. Focus the mind and hold the tension. Think of it. Now begin, slowly, to relax and release. Let the buttocks loosen slowly. Feel the relief flooding into the buttocks as they loosen and relax and you sink lazily on to the floor.

Move your mind up to your stomach. Sense a gradual tension coming into the stomach. Tense it slowly. Your breathing will become shallow and virtually non-existent as your stomach muscles tighten. You will be aware of a tense and quiet stillness in your body. Expel all the air from your lungs in quiet little gasps of expulsion. When no air is left, your stomach muscles will be taut. The whole abdominal area will be tense and still. Keep the mind focused on the stomach muscle. The tension will halt all breathing. The thoracic cavity will be still. Focus on the stillness and the tension.

Then relax your stomach muscles totally. As you release them, you will experience a steady and natural running of air back into the depth of your lungs. Let it run its course and fill naturally. Feel the lungs expand, the stomach muscles lift as they distend from the gentle pressure of the air finding its way back into your lungs. Let your breath return to normal. Lie at ease and at peace. Feel the natural quiet of your breathing find its own easy rhythm. Slowly start to tense the muscles of the stomach again. Let the air out in small gasps. Feel the stomach muscles tighten as the air puffs out. Go through the above process once more. Be aware of the difference in tension and release from it. Keep the mind on it.

If your mind wanders, bring it back with a quiet determination to where you're working. Hold it there and keep it focused. Be calm and relentless in your concentration. The body will respond to your thought direction. You will experience relaxation at its most delicate intensity.

The next set deals with the upper body; arms and chest area. Gently roll your hands into a fist. Begin to tighten them, feeling the tension in your hands and forearms. Gradually increase the tension. Raise the forearms off the floor until they are perpendicular from the elbow. Keep the tension in the fists. Now begin to press the elbows into your sides. Keep the elbows on the floor. Keep pressing the elbows into the sides and on to the floor. Feel your chest tighten as well. Hold the tension. As you hold this tension, you will notice it manifesting itself in other ways. Your breathing will become slightly faster. It will also be more shallow. The tension you experience in this hold will be very similar to what happens you physically when you are anxious or stressed. The same effects will be apparent to you as you tense your elbows into your sides. There is a sense of constriction in the chest which inhibits respiration. These effects can be self-perpetuating and unless conscious steps are taken to break them down, can have serious effects on the body.

Now, having held this tension for long enough to experience these feelings, slowly let it go. Feel the relief flooding into your chest, your sides, your arms and even your shoulders. You will probably mark the total release of tension with a deep sigh, letting the lungs draw long and deep and your breathing return to a settled rhythm, at the same time letting your forearms lie along the floor as before, letting everything go, letting the hands lie, palms upwards, letting the fingers find their own comfortable position in looseness and ease, with your knuckles lying quietly on the floor.

Now relax. Stay loose. Close your eyes. Be aware of the ease of your breathing as your body unwinds. Isn't that word so appropriate? Imagine it. To unwind. All the tightness in your system is letting go. The tension is leaving and you are becoming a dead weight. Imagine it. You are so loose in your feet, your legs, your waist and your chest, in your arms and your shoulders that you are unable to move. You don't want to move. You are loose and relaxed, quiet, still. Your mind is focused only on the ease and the looseness of your body. Your body is responding by lying lazily on the floor. It is heavy and loose and at ease and at rest. So is your mind. It sees the depth of the quiet to which you have drifted. You are deeply and calmly quiet, inside yourself, aware of the stillness of your mind and body. Your mind is drifting gently with the peace and tranquillity which suffuses your body. All is still but for your breathing. This is slow and rhythmic, the gentlest of movements, giving peace to the rest of your body. The flow of your breath is like the quiet tide of life, flowing and ebbing in the gentle strength of relentless nature, filling your mind and body with the calm force of imperturbable tranquillity. For it is here that your strength will grow. This is the source of your life.

Now let yourself rest at ease. Permit your mind to let your body sink and sink and sink, so you sink and drift deeply into further quiet and further warmth and deep, deep stillness. You may lie like this for a while. With practice the time will become longer. And easier. Though the length is not all that important. What really matters is the quality and the frequency of your relaxation sessions.

When you've experienced the depth of relaxation you can begin to move again, slowly. Shift your feet. Move your legs. Lift and bend your arms. Clench and open your fists. Roll the head and shrug the shoulders. You will be surprised at the consciousness of movement as you come out of your quiet entrancement.

Sit up slowly. Then rise and stretch. You will be much more aware of life in your limbs, particularly the stretching, as you begin to move about again. You will also find that you will be less tense and stiff, but calmly alert to what is going on around you and how you fit into things in general. One pupil of mine put it very succinctly when he described the difference the practice of daily relaxation made to his day-to-day living. 'It was as if the frenzy left my life,' he said. It sums up the reaction of most people.

Because of the intense personal nature of this practice, you can see the necessity for observing the ground rules. Quiet, privacy and constancy are the key elements in the success of this journey. For that is what this is. It is a journey within yourself and within your own potential. For whatever purpose in life you may have, this practise will equip you the focus and the the quiet determination to complete any thing you start. It will open the doors of imagination and initiative that may never before have presented themselves to you.

Do it every day of your life. That means Saturdays and Sundays too. Let it become a part of your everyday living. Do not deny yourself this opportunity. Do it wherever you are, whether your'e in the Bahamas, in Ireland, in prison or hospital.

6

THE MAGIC OF DIET

Given the thousands of words written on diet, I've no intention of adding anything here. But let's condense and see if we can make practical suggestions. You can read books and articles forever and end up little the wiser about what to do. So what's important at this stage is to learn a few principles, a few basic facts about yourself and about food. Don't switch off because someone once blinded you with science and made it all sound very deep and difficult.

There are simple facts about food which anyone of average intelligence can understand. Know these and you'll be able to determine whether you're going to be fit or fat, or unwell.

Here's the first thing to know; when you look in the mirror you see a solid mass, don't you? Now consider this; everything in every thing you see is made up of tiny cells, invisible to the naked eye. Every part and organ of your body is made of millions and millions of these tiny cells.

They are constantly coming into existence, existing and then dying. Your skin, your eyes, your hair, teeth, are all made up of these cells. The condition of your body is thus dependent on the condition of your cells. So if you look after the nourishment and welfare of your cells, you'll have healthy skin, teeth, eyes, hair, muscle and so on. In other words, your body will be in good condition and you will function efficiently.

All the cells in your body, brain cells, nerve cells, blood cells, everything in your system, must have two ingredients for a healthy existence: oxygen and nutrition. The oxygen we get from the air we breathe; the nutrition we get from the food we eat. So when someone tells you you are what you eat, you know he's right. Give the cells of each body part what they need and you'll have healthy tissue in each part, and your body, your mind and emotions will function more efficiently as a whole.

It can be as simple as that, so don't complicate it. Eat the right foods, and not too much, and you'll be supplying the various cells which go to make up your body with the materials which will help maintain them in good condition. Your body has its own miraculous way of sorting out and distributing the right materials to the appropriate places. Nature is a great organiser.

However if you persist in eating wrong foods, and too much, you'll rob your body of the ingredients necessary to keep it well while overloading the system with surplus and waste. Toxins will build up and poison the body. Fat will accumulate and wear you down. You'll end up being over-fed and undernourished. There's a lot of that today. But it's easily rectified. All you have to do is make sure you are getting wholefoods at your grocer's. Fruit and vegetables are largely very fresh today and can be got anywhere. They're also cleaner than they were years ago and much more appetisingly presented. There is also a greater variety than even a decade ago so you can pick and choose and enjoy a good selection.

By contrast, quite a few of the convenience foods, by contrast, have few, if any, of the nutrients we need to keep healthy and well. A lot of tinned foods, packet foods, frozen fast foods, lack the essential ingredients to help the growth and maintenance of the cells. It's often the lack of nutrients which contributes to the run-down feeling, the lack of energy, low resistance to colds and flu, and even ill-humour and depression. For instance, research has shown that people who lack the B-vitamins in their bodies tend to be more nervous, irritable and out of form than those who are adequately supplied with this vitamin.

The pace of life today has a lot to do with our modern diet. Everything is done in a rush. Meals are no exception. We eat in a hurry because we have to be here, there and everywhere else at the same time. Most people today eat on the run. It's reflected in our language; we 'grab' a sandwich, 'gulp' a cup of tea, 'take a snack' en route to somewhere. We've lost the habit of sitting and eating because we need to or want to. Working breakfasts are commonplace. And God help us, there are even power breakfasts now. How would you like that? Not only do you have to work at your breakfast but you must exhibit power as well!

Let's look at the body first.

God, or your dentist, gave you teeth for a few good reasons. The main function we're aware of is to bite and chew. Most of the foods we eat are solids. They are meant to be chewed, masticated, worked to a pulp, before being swallowed into the digestive system. When they go down into the stomach they are further broken down by the digestive juices, absorbed into the bloodstream as the materials of growth and repair for the cells and finally assimilated into the tissue of which we are composed.

If we don't chew our food adequately, lumps of solid food are thrown into a poor unsuspecting stomach, which is then asked to do what should have been done by the teeth. Needless to say, there is a delay in the process. Nature has different intentions and is not going to be regimented by the hurly-burly of modern society. Accordingly, she takes her time and proceeds to do what she can with the unchewed food. In the meantime, we're swallowing more unchewed food, rushing around in a state of hypertension and generally behaving in a way that is going to result in one of today's common disorders: indigestion.

Not only do we not chew our foods adequately but we compound the problem by eating and drinking together. The digestive system is in confusion. It can't function efficiently. The food can't be used properly. The system is overloaded. It has to take whatever action is necessary to defend itself against the onslaught of excess.

A number of things which should be happening are not, and a number of things which should not be happening are. Rushed and unchewed food can result in indigestion, wind, constipation, spots, boils, fatigue and irritability. It also has a big part to play in overweight. Most excess weight comes from excess food and drink. Hurried eating prevents the message of satisfaction getting to the brain before the excess food gets taken in. And even relatively small excesses, three times a day, accumulate. The consequence is too much food in the body, more than we need, getting stored as fat.

Apart from the weight aspect, if we expect our digestive processes to work properly, we have to give them a chance. So start by chewing your food. Bite it well, chew it thoughtfully. Take small mouthfuls, eaten slowly, chewed well. This practice also extends the time given to eating and makes the whole affair of a meal or even a snack more leisurely. Taking the hurry out of eating can relax the body mind as well. The digestive system will work more efficiently and use what food you do eat the way nature intended.

Research has shown that tension shows not only in how you feel, but in how your system works. When you are tense, nervous, or wound up in preparation or anticipation, you're not going to digest anything you eat, so either wait till the occasion is over before eating or eat small amounts, chew it very well, and wait till you've swallowed your chewed solids before drinking anything.

The foregoing paragraphs have to do with you, how you take food, what happens once the food goes into you and what you can expect from how you eat it. As in everything else it's not only what you do, it's how you do it.

That goes for excercise, breathing, rest and diet.

If your diet is healthy, regular and sound in vitamin content, it's all the more important to observe how you eat it to maximise on the quality of what you're eating. Some people dismiss this as being unnecessary, as if it's giving undue importance to some fussy details.

But if you're going to go to the trouble of examining what's going into you, it makes sense to maximise on the machinery or chemistry used in the activity, doesn't it? Food is not just solid. Food can be liquid. Milk is food. Soup is food. Meat is food. Coffee is a drug. Coffee with milk and sugar is a food.

Let's examine this. If it seems confusing at first, bear with it. There are a few simple principles which will clarify the main matters relating to our day-to-day existence. It is generally accepted that the science of nutrition is the study of the growth, maintenance and repair of the human body from the use of the nutrients given by the food we eat.

One class of food helps the growth, maintenance and repair of all human cells. This we call protein. Other classes are needed as a source of energy for body chemistry and life to take place. These are fats and carbohydrates (sugars, starches). Others again are needed to make sure that the growth and health of cells are regulated and that the production of energy is regulated. These are called vitamins, minerals and trace elements.

111

We need an adequate daily intake of protein - about 75–90 grams, in order for growth and repair to take place. This might constitute 10–20 per cent of the daily calorific intake. We need 50–60 per cent of our intake from natural carbo-hydrates - fruit, vegetables. We could do with under 30 per cent of our daily intake as fat. We also need to ensure that we get fresh fruits and vegatables for their vitamin and mineral content.

There is a way to simplify all this without going into encyclopaedic detail.

Most of the foods eaten today are high in sugar and starch and fat. It gives a flavour which develops as a sweet tooth and a texture which develops a yearning for these foods. Chocolates, sweets, ices, cakes, scones, pastries, various breads, cereals, tinned and packaged foods come under these headings. The problem can be eating these to the exclusion of fresh or wholesome foods.

It is not necessary to live a life of deprivation and anxiety over everything you eat. Just adjust the balance. Think about this. If the tendency at the moment is towards too much sugary, starchy fast food, and you eat only the occasional fresh food, and if your cooked food is mainly fried, accompanied by slices of hot toast drenched in butter and washed down with big sweet mugs of tea, there's a fair chance that your weight may be a bit more than you'd like, and your fitness may be a bit less than it could be. A run for a bus, a climb up a stairs, carrying a heavy object will soon show up this lack of fitness.

It's also possible you may have a snack habit, where every cup of tea brings with it a biscuit (or three) or a bar or a sandwich. A lot of these foods are unsatisfying. They tend to bloat without satisfaction so that a short time later, you can be peckish again. More tea and biscuits follow. The snacks and sweets and bars become habit. The circle is established. It doesn't seem as if a lot of food is going in at any one time, and here lies a big part of the problem.

Two or three biscuits are consumed in minutes. So is a bar. Or a sandwich. As individual snacks they don't amount to much. But at the end of a day they add up. They can be low in protein and vitually devoid of vitamins, minerals, trace elements. What gets fed is the fat, what gets deprived is the body. The fat builds up, adding weight, misaligning the posture, making the breathing difficult and shallow, slowing the circulation down. The person affected becomes tired and run-down, prone to illness, weak and lethargic. Because the vital organs and components of the body, heart, muscle, blood and bones, are not being fed properly, they suffer under the strain of too little nutrient and too much food. So even though the person may be eating too much, s/he may still be suffering from malnutrition.

But a balance can be struck. We've spoken about the ingestion of sweets, pastries and all these goodies with high fat, high sugar content and few or no valuable nutrients. A simple process of change will alter everything for the good.

If, for example, your own daily snack habits amount to two bars, six biscuits and an ice-cream, you may think there isn't really much you can cut down on. After all you'd eat a bar on the way to work, another one on the way home, and nibble a few biscuits at tea-breaks or after dinner. A choc-ice, or another bar could quietly disappear during *Coronation Street.*

But from Friday to Monday that makes ten to fifteen bars of chocolate, twenty-five to thirty-five biscuits, and that isn't counting any scones (hot with butter and jam!), Danish pastries, sweet drinks, sandwiches and crisps that might be taken on board along the way. If you decided to even the balance, halving the chocolate, halving the biscuits, or better, cutting them out and replacing them with fruit, you'll be doing a couple of things from which your health, weight and wellbeing will benefit.

Firstly, you'll be diminishing hugely the weekly intake of fat and sugar. You'll lose excess pounds and not so slowly either. Secondly, you'll be getting vitamins and minerals from your fruits and vegetables. Your metabolism, while getting rid of the fat, toxins and wastes that have built up over the months or the years, will also help the functioning of blood, muscle, nervous system, digestive system and eliminative system. Because of this you'll sleep better, have more energy and feel a lot better. Thirdly, you'll be giving your system a supply of natural roughage, so your body will excrete other toxins and wastes that would previously have silted up inside you.

You'll be leaner and fitter. Your body will react more vigorously to your breathing regime and your excercises. Physical activity will increase hugely in value. Your metabolism and circulation, instead of having to cope with excess baggage and keep the system clean for normal day-to-day living, will now be able to work on the maintenance and repair of your cells.

You will have more vitality. Your vigour and ability to apply yourself will soar. You will find yourself with the desire and the means to do the things you want to do in life. You will be healthier and happier. As well as alterating your snacking habits, it will help if you make sure to regulate your eating patterns. Group your day into eating times. Develop a pattern you follow. If it means taking food with you, do that.

Harmful eating patterns come about because they're allowed to. Good ones can be just as easily developed. A pattern of two or three meals a day will become a habit. A meal doesn't have to be a big plate of meat, vegetables and potatoes. It can be a sandwich and a cup of soup. It can be an apple. Or it can be a full dinner.

Some people eat a full breakfast, a dinner at lunchtime, and a fry-up with plenty of bread at dinnertime. For a lot of people in today's world this would be just too much food, unless they were extraordinarily active or had a metabolism which burned off food as it went in.

If you find you're carrying a few pounds or a few stone that you could do without, examine what you're taking on a day-to-day basis. Write it all down as you eat it. I say this because most of us are wonders of self-deception and will not admit to ourselves what we're taking. It's like a denial of responsibility. We give ourselves excuses like, 'We're all big our family'; 'I'm big boned'; 'It's my metabolism', rather than say to ourselves, I'm eating too much and the wrong kinds of food.'

Apart from weight, the vital thing to keep in mind is our health. By modifying our use of food from poor to useful, we'll be making a decent contribution to our resistance to colds and flu and other types of illness. This is really the priority of eating well. You can affect the change by looking at the lists of foods at the end of this chapter. See whether the balance is in favour of the recommended foods or the ones to have less of, and start making the appropriate choices.

Most people are surprised to find how easy it is to make the change. Once they've said no to the chocolate bar or biscuit habit a couple of times, it comes very easily to keep easily to keep on the right track with a growing reluctance to allow anything to jeopardise it.

So do start to write the list of what you're eating on a daily basis. It may be a real eye-opener for you. It is for others. Don't bother getting guilty or making yourself give up every sugary or sweet thing you eat. Just do this first as an excercise in observation. Then, if you've a mind to change how you feel, get rid of some excess weight or help yourself to safeguard your health, go to the lists at the end and start weighing the balance in favour of the recommended foods.

One point. If you're doing the list, write it as you eat. Don't, don't, don't put off making a note of it at the time. The object of the excercise is to help yourself see what's going into your system over a few days.

A lot of people get enough information in just one or two days. The habits which they'd expected become apparent and they take the necessary steps to rectify the matter. Once you're into a good habit and you begin to see results you'll find it easy to perpetuate the system. And please don't imagine that you've to forego any treats for the rest of your life. Such a notion would be the one certain way of ensuring that you never even get started right.

Now you'll see why the breathing excercises are so important. It's the oxygen we get into our bloodstream that helps to transmute the food nutrients into healthy body tissue. The oxygen also takes away the waste of unused food and dead tissue. This also shows the significance of abdominal breathing and complete exhalation. Every breath helps to improve the health and vitality of our bodies.

A point here on the quality of food; it's been said that it doesn't matter how much you eat, what matters is what you eat. There is a provision here. Even the best and most nutritious of food will have the effect of building waste, overweight, and associated disadvantages if you eat too much of it. That's a fact of life. Some people imagine a life of continuous gorging with no ill-effects because they're eating recommended food.

Whatever you eat, eat well but no more than you need. That's easier said than done. But if you do develop the habit of chewing you'll find it a great help. You'll savour what you are eating more as well as getting more benefit from it. So taking it for granted that you're being fairly moderate in the amounts you eat, the foods from which you're going to benefit for the structural welfare of your body are fish, poultry, lean meats, eggs and very moderate amounts of cheese and milk. These are used in the maintenance work of the body. And of course we need other ingredients to help the body chemistry do its work.

If you take in less food, without any increase in activity, you'll lose some weight and feel better. If you increase your activity considerably and maintain your food intake, you'll also lose a bit of weight, and you'll feel better. But, if you increase your activity lightly but constantly, lessen moderately, while choosing prudently what you eat and drink, you will lose weight, reshape your body, tone and revitalise your whole system, and look, feel and be immeasurably better.

Again, it's not what you're doing so much as how you're doing it.

There are people who would say, 'Oh, I see, so it's just diet 'n' excercise.' Yes, both of these regimes are used but it's a bit more than that. It's a matter of attitude. Some people might approach the whole thing with an attitude that has all the life of a brick wall. Written on their faces, spoken silently with their hunched shoulders and hung head, is the declaration of defeat. 'I know this won't work,' is written in their demeanour. And of course they're right. It won't. Like the team who wonder in the changing room how much they're going to be beaten by, their only concern is how badly they will fail.

A peculiar thing is this. I've seen people who've approached the course in this manner. Their attitude predicted failure. For various reasons, failure had been their constant experience. They had become accustomed to it, even comfortable in it. Having a goal, an aim, an ambition involved risk; risk of failure, fear of rejection, fear of ridicule, fear of change, and worst of all, fear of success. Not a few people feel they're unworthy of their dream. You've heard the saying, 'It's too good to be true', all too often uttered by misguided people who believe that success in any undertaking, financial, physical, spiritual, is not compatible with reality.

Our negative conditioning is so forceful that there is a fear of success and a guilt about attaining it. Watch this. Think about it. If this applies to you, no matter how hard you strive, how cleverly you operate, no matter what refinement of intelligence you bring to your efforts, you'll still do things to sabotage your attempts.

We're back to the point at the beginning of the book: know, see, feel, dream about what you want to be and to feel. This is your life. Provided you're not transgressing the laws or rights of others, you can do what you want with your life. It's no one else's business. Again, this is why it is important to keep your aims to yourself and to imbue your own mind with them. Particularly at this time when they're new, shaky, not altogether clear and very vulnerable. Don't expose them to malicious attack or to ridicule. Let them settle. Let them become clear in your mind. Develop them till they are unshakeable objectives, a very part of your life. Then, unlike the case of the person hypnotised by failure, your subconscious will have you activating the opportunities to achieve the images in your mind.

So where does this come into dietary habits? Simply that we can all be masters of self-deception. We will tell ourselves we're big-boned, overweight by heredity, just in need of a bit more exercise and any number of other much more imaginative excuses. True, some people do have a tendency to overweight. It is also true that a few, a very few, are overweight due to glandular malfunction, while it's also true that some people are heavily boned and heavily muscled.

But for a start, glandular problems usually arise from either the overweight or nutritional imbalance anyway, and then the cycle perpetuates itself. Big bones and heavy muscle may be present in anyone, but it's the fold of flesh round the stomach, chest or hips or waist that's being excused, not the bone and muscle.

Let's look at it squarely. Faulty eating is the main culprit in obesity. Eating practices can be improved. Now, along with the protein bearing foods we've mentioned, it's important to have a source of energy for life processes to take place and for daily activity. The best and most natural sources of energy are fruits, vegetables, and some cereals and breads. A variety of these foods, eaten fresh and lightly cooked, will help to ensure a source of the other vital ingredients: vitamins, minerals and trace elements. These are needed only in small amounts but their absence will result in poor efficiency of the chemical processes of the body and symptoms as varied as a mild decline in appetite, a ravenous desire for sweets, chronic headaches, fatigue, susceptibility to colds or nervous depression.

One sure way of getting your vitamin/mineral requirements is to take a good multi-vitamin/mineral tablet every day. This will have the Recommended Daily Requirement of every vitamin and mineral and means that you will maximise on the other foods you are eating. Your body chemistry, supplied with the necessary ingredients, and enough oxygen from your breathing and excercise habits, will now be able to function the way nature intended.

What's more you will be working steadily from the inside out, not just losing a few inches and pounds but creating the basis for lifelong trim health and vitality.

If you make the changes recommended, put the emphasis on the foods indicated, while keeping an eye for the ones you're advised to keep low, you'll bring about a remarkable change in your wellbeing over a few months. You don't have to live like a spartan. Just edge the trend in the right direction. Your body will take care of the rest.

And don't go mad on the weighing scales every half-hour; you'll only drive yourself insane. Just decide you're going to eat well, not too much, and let the rest happen. It will. Don't have a fit because you might be a pound or two heavier one day than a day or two previously. Body weight fluctuates all the time. If you decide that you're going to eat what you know will contribute to good health and a trim figure, you can even forget about weighing scales. Once you've got to a satisfactory shape and condition you can maintain it simply enough. If you find your waistband tightening, your slacks getting too snug on the thighs, make a few modifications, stick to your decision and give it the time. Keeping results is a lot less difficult than most people think. Once patterns have been established they tend to stay that way.

Have a look at the following lists. Without going to extremes, give yourself less of the foods to beware of. There are some, marked with an asterisk, which you could cut out entirely at the start, as they're high in fat or starches or sugars, or all three, and also tend not to have any quality nutrients to help you to health.

One point to bear in mind; quite a few of the foods on the first list have alternative diet versions which are as tasty. In some cases too they are fortified with extra vitamins. Use these if you wish.

Start the habit of reading labels. All manufacturers are obliged now to state the nutritional composition of their products. These are usually given per 100 grams or per helping. It's very simple to start determining how much fat you're eating, how much carbohydrate and how much protein. You can very simply take charge of your diet these days. And it isn't expensive to eat well, certainly no dearer than some of the rubbish-laden meals that pass for a diet.

USE SPARINGLY OR OMIT COMPLETELY

Anything fried
Alcohol*
Bacon
Biscuits
Bread
Breakfast cereals
Buns
Butter*
Cakes
Chips
Chocolates
Cocoa
Cornflour
Crisps
Custard
Doughnuts
Dumplings
Flour
Ice-cream*
Jams*
Jelly
Macaroni

Macaroons
Margarine*
Mayonnaise*
Milk
Muffins
Pastries
Peanuts
Pies
Pork
Potatoes fried or with butter
Puddings
Rice (fried)
Sauces
Sausages
Scones
Shortbread
Spaghetti
Sugar
Sweets
Tarts
Tinned fruit
Toast
Soft drinks*

USE THESE INSTEAD

Any fresh fruit, or stewed if you wish
Any vegetable, raw or lightly cooked
Bran
Boiled/baked potato
Chicken and other poultry (skin taken off)
Fish
Lean meats

Eggs (boiled/poached/scrambled)
Wholewheat bread
Cottage cheese
Low fat cheese
Water
Coffee/tea with a little milk, no sugar
Low fat milk on bran/wholewheat cereals
Low fat yoghurt
Low fat margarines or butters very thinly spread

GROUND RULES FOR HEALTHY EATING

1 Chew very well.
2 Eat and drink separately – sip fluids between mouthfuls or after you've eaten.
3 Use fruit first on its own – not as part of a meal.
4 Allow time to eat in a leisurely way – do take the time for quiet and peace when you're eating. Either leave the work environment or take the phone off the hook or put on your answering machine.
5 Eat nothing fried.
6 Get into the habit of checking labels and information on packets and tins. It's interesting and informative.
7 Do try to stop eating when you feel you've had what you need.
8 If you must snack, choose fruit or vegetables.
9 Use a good multi-vitamin/mineral tablet.
10 Practise breathing exercises as prescribed to help metabolise the good foods you're now using.

ALCOHOL

Alcohol is a drug. Socially, in the context of loosening up and being with people, it can be used constructively. But everybody's reaction to it is different. And different people respond differently to types of drink. As far as weight is concerned, it can be instrumental in piling it on.

Ideally, we'd probably all be better off without it, but it's not an ideal world. Alcohol use and abuse is a fact of life. How you let it affect your life is your own choice.

It's a drug. It affects your nervous system and your brain in the short term, and God knows what else in the long term.

Tread cautiously.

7

HYGIENE

There is a story about the celebrated eighteenth-century writer and wit, Dr Samuel Johnson, that not only indicates his speed of thought and mastery of words but has a bearing on a situation which applies in today's society.

The doctor was a guest at a party where he had the place of honour and it was to be a high point for some of the guests to be introduced to the great man and thereby be able to claim a personal friendship. As the writer was not famous for his personal hygiene (he suffered from what is euphemistically described today as BO) a few people were shocked. Yet because of his social and literary stature, they concealed their dismay, uttered sycophantic noises and retreated. One lady, though, so overcome by the surprise exclaimed, 'Why Dr Johnson, you smell!' The Doctor, in what must have been an audible silence, not only saved the party and his reputation but brilliantly enhanced both with the reply: 'Not true, Madam. It is you who smell. I stink.'

Which brings us to the subject of hygiene, or lack of it. While a good number of people today take showers with encouraging regularity, there are still those who labour under the misapprehension that it isn't necessary to take a bath, or a good overall wash, provided they haven't been playing hurling or football for one and a half hours.

You only have to sit in a bus, stand in a queue or wander round a department store to experience personally the existence of the 'great unwashed'. This can apply to anyone. You can get the smell of stale sweat from a hand-fashioned wool suit or from a sweater and jeans.

Everybody sweats. Never doubt it. All normally healthy people sweat continuously. What differs is the degree and intensity. People who don't take excercise, eat the wrong foods and take too many stimulants such as tea and coffee will sweat fairly profusely. People who are fairly fit and keep an eye on the stimulants will sweat but less copiously.

When sweat dries it lies on the body and on the clothes in immediate contact with it. Then it smells. A five-minute shower will solve the problem. Deodorants are no substitute for a good overall wash and rinse. They're only any good at all if the body is already fresh and clean. Deodorants applied to an unwashed body not only make the problem of odour worse, they form a heavier layer of chemicals with the existing sweat and interfere with the natural elimination processes of the pores.

With the speed of life today, the stresses and tensions, it is advisable to develop the daily shower habit. You'll feel better and your neighbours and colleagues will appreciate it.

FINALLY...

The foregoing pages will only be as good as the use to which you put them. Once you've read them through, which I assume you've done if you're this far, reread the book with a pen or pencil. Mark the particular exercises or dietary facts which seem relevant to your needs and devise a suitable personal course from the exercises and recom-mend-ations that you intend to put into practice. You will take to some exercises very quickly while you will have to push yourself a bit to do the others. Above all do them regularly and complement the physical activity with the breathing movements which will develop your lung capacity and assist your posture. This in turn will help you apply yourself more vigorously to the other parts of your programme, as you will be keen not to jeopardise any success by creating a weak link.

Plan to read three to five pages a day. You may well be surprised that on rereading you will come across perceptions you'll have missed earlier. The rereading will make a course out of the information in the book. You will find that this system will help you to absorb the more important points into your mind. You will get a better overall picture of the system and see it much more clearly in relation to your own needs. As with any kind of course, there will be parts which appeal to you more than others. Rereading helps to integrate all the parts in your mind. It will also stimulate your thinking as how best to apply the various elements in your own life and what you want to achieve from the whole process.

Your aims will change. As you reach one goal, another will reveal itself to you. But don't worry about that now. Just think of the thing you want to achieve at this stage and don't panic if it doesn't come about exactly as you wished. Fate and Faith have strange ways of working. Your success in your life need not be measured in terms of material acquisition, though there's nothing wrong in that, but in achieving what you set out to do. Sometimes, the gain may be different from the aim, but the shift from the starting point is as successful.

Thought is the helm by which you steer on a course of success or failure. Often the avoidance of failure is success in itself. A goal, an aim, however tenuous, will give course to your life. A defined, clarified, articulated aim can set your life alight. The worst that can happen is that you may not achieve it. And God knows what you might achieve and learn along the way.

Go back to the beginning. Write what you want to be or to do or to have. And then keep it in your mind. It's the sense of purpose which gives meaning to what you do. The purpose of this book is to help you towards the life, vitality and sheer enjoyment of day-to-day living

The old dicta still prevail. If you choose to live with faith in yourself, hope in your spirit, charity to the world, you will be laying a foundation for whatever quest you may pursue.

I wish you every success and every happiness in whatever that may be.

Start with that thought.